A CULINARY HISTORY OF
MYRTLE BEACH & THE GRAND STRAND

Fish & Grits, Oyster Roasts and Boiled Peanuts

BECKY BILLINGSLEY

AMERICAN PALATE

Published by American Palate
A Division of The History Press
Charleston, SC 29403
www.historypress.net

First published 2013

Manufactured in the United States

ISBN 978.1.60949.956.3

Library of Congress CIP data applied for.

CONTENTS

FOREWORD

Native American people are and have been very influential in building this nation. I know there were tough times—I have not forgotten the wars and raids—but our contributions to the settlers, especially on the East Coast, by far overshadow any hostilities.

Without the Native American influence, this country's history would only span 237 years, if the settlers survived at all. We taught them what, where and how to plant; how and what to hunt; and even how to prepare their meals when they reaped the fruits of our land.

History is not fair to all concerned, and neither is it always accurate. However, right or wrong, it is history. For these and a few other reasons, I am honored to write this foreword.

I am always willing to talk about my people, my tribe, my heritage and my children. I am very proud of all of them. My mother, whom I hope was proud of me, taught me lots of things. She didn't do it in some formal setting; she just did things and I learned.

This was how I learned to preserve tubers through a winter. Mother made us dig a hole and fill it with pine straw. Then we put the vegetables on the straw and piled on more pine straw. Lastly, we covered the whole thing over with dirt. The dirt insulated the vegetables from the cold winter air so they didn't freeze. The pine straw disguised the smell so even the local wild hogs and rodents wouldn't dig them up. The straw underneath the tubers kept the vegetables from taking root or rotting, and I believe the pine smell kept a lot of bugs at bay as well. I didn't know it then, but these "potato banks" were the way natives preserved their tubers through the winter.

Native Americans in the Grand Strand area used digging sticks in their gardens, such as this one on display at the Horry County Museum in Conway. *Photo by Matt Silfer, Silfer Studios.*

Mama always said a blessing before we ate. She learned about prayers through exposure to the Christians who are predominant in our area. Most of my people today are Christian, but for me, the ancient spiritual practices feel better. Instead of a blessing before a meal, our people would share their food with the earth to thank the Creator for it. We would take a small portion, offer it to the seven directions and then place it outside for the animals to eat. I practice that, and it feels right for me.

So, Indian culture is alive and well in South Carolina, and I want it to stay that way. I want it preserved, and I am smart enough to know that if it is to survive, it has to be documented. So, when Ms. Billingsley asked for my help in including the native aspect in her book, I readily agreed.

I take the culture seriously, and I didn't want it to be just a passing thought or a surface interest. I wanted her to see, taste and know the food, as well as write about it, so I invited her to meet a few of my members, all of whom I knew cooked some traditional dishes.

I also invited her to our tribal office and to some of our gatherings. I even provided her with contact information for a traditional native spiritualist so she might learn some of the herbs we used to treat illnesses and the spiritual aspects of the healing practices. She came! She saw! She learned!

Then she learned how native foods influenced the diets of those who came later, like European immigrants and African slaves, and how many traditionally southern foods we enjoy to this day are rooted in Native American history.

Before you begin reading, I would like to offer a blessing: May you walk on clear paths beneath a blue sky as your moccasins walk softly across life's many journeys.

–Chief Harold D. "Buster" Hatcher of the Waccamaw People

ACKNOWLEDGEMENTS

To all the people of Horry and Georgetown Counties who deliciously share with others their culinary experiences, wisdom and recipes; authors whose work was included in this collection of local food history; and those who oversee our local history documentation. Thank you for preserving our past.

INTRODUCTION

Fish and grits, chicken bog, duck pilau and boiled peanuts were once thought of as subsistence foods in the Grand Strand area, but these days, they're considered more a type of comfort cuisine and a way to connect to the area's deep and flavorful roots.

Heritage cuisine has come full circle in recent years in this bountiful area of the Carolina coast. What attracted Native Americans like the Waccamaw and Chicora People to set up camps along the rivers and make fishing trips to the beaches are the same reasons some 15 million visitors come here each year: the weather is great and the food is even better.

Those Native Americans—and then Spanish explorers followed by European immigrants—savored the same basic foods we relish today. The salty-sweet brine of our unique cluster oysters; the intoxicating, earthy smell of freshly ground corn; the delicate chewiness and slight popcorn aroma of fresh Carolina Gold rice; and the sassy fire of fish stew are parts of the natives' collective memory. Factor in a long growing season, with plenty of time for abundant crops of tomatoes, squash, sweet potatoes, peanuts, pears, figs, berries and so much more, and it's easy to understand why current generations are getting back to basics.

Myrtle Beach still has plenty of fast-food restaurants and Calabash seafood buffets, but there is a resurgence among chefs and home cooks to grow their own food or seek farm-fresh products at the area's many farmers' markets and produce stands. Some, especially those in the more outlying parts of the Grand Strand, never forgot their culinary heritage. They have always made neckbone gravy and rice thickened with minced hardboiled egg, stuffed their own sausages and scored fresh flounder before deep-frying it. A majority of similar recipes are common across ethnicity and race—they became everyone's foods.

Some of those keepers of the culinary faith are home cooks, and others own restaurants. We owe all of them much gratitude for cooking extraordinary food and showing new generations how to prepare fresh, local harvests the way their granddaddies and great-great-grandmothers did, sinking culinary roots even deeper to reach new heights of creative flavors.

Chapter 1
NEW WORLD

South Carolina Indian tribes didn't see themselves as all that much different from one another, especially if they spoke the same language.

"You couldn't tell the difference between [South Carolina] tribes with a blood test," Chief Harold D. "Buster" Hatcher said. He has been the leader of the Waccamaw Indian People since the group was officially founded in 1992.

In fact, the Waccamaw Indians didn't even call themselves that until white settlers came along and pinned the name on them. They saw Indians living along the Waccamaw River in Georgetown and Horry Counties, so they called them Waccamaw Indians. The word "Waccamaw," Chief Hatcher said, means "the river that comes and goes," because strong tides near the coast make the current switch direction.

In addition to the Waccamaw People, the Grand Strand area was home to the Chicora Indian People near Pawleys Island and the Sewees in lower Georgetown County. The Santee Indians were a bit more to the west toward Orangeburg County, while the Winyahs lived around Winyah Bay, the Black River and the Lower Pee Dee River in Georgetown County.

Chief Clyde Strickland of the Chicora Indian People said that Chicora was a nation with many tribes. He estimated that before 1521, when the first Spanish explorers arrived in the Grand Strand area, there were "thousands upon thousands" of Native Americans.

All those tribes, and many others around the Southeast that traveled in and out of the area, spoke a language called Siouan. They had no written language or records until the late eighteenth century. "A village would consist probably of 100 to 150 people. Pee Dee villages, the Waccamaw People, they were all the same people," Chief Hatcher said. "They hunted together. Their only enemies were the Cherokee and Tuscarora, because they didn't speak the same language, so they were 'evil.'"

In about 8000 BC, South Carolina Indians stopped being nomadic and began settling down, at least seasonally. By 1000 BC, small villages had begun to form with the building of curved-top dwellings called suks. "They had to rebuild them about every two years," Chief Hatcher said. "They had villages, sometimes even with palisades."

Wild game was a primary source of protein. Deer were plentiful, and sometimes after a doe was hunted and eaten, her fawns were domesticated and then the Indians drank their milk and made cheese from it. However, it was likely not a conventional hard cheese because the humid Grand Strand climate is not dry and even enough to produce great cheeses, according to Horry County Museum director Walter Hill. He said that it's more likely the Indian cheese was a type of clabber, with the whey skimmed off to make a sort of crème fraîche.

The skies were thick with fowl, often to the point that the sun was obliterated by great flocks of migrating ducks. The Indians used spears, arrows, nets, traps and rakes to harvest turkeys, geese, turtles, muskrats, bears, beaver, fresh and saltwater fish, crabs, oysters and more. Chief Strickland said that buffalo roamed eastern South Carolina before the 1500s and were an important food source.

Evidence of their love of oysters dots the Carolina coast in the form of huge mounds of cast-off oyster and clamshells called middens, left behind by seasonal Indian encampments. Belle W. Baruch Foundation senior interpreter Lee Brockington said that most of the middens in the areas around Hobcaw Barony, Pawleys Island and Litchfield are made of clamshells, which is a recent discovery by Dr. Chester Depratter and Dr. Paul Brockington Jr. "And why is the question that begs the answer," Brockington said. "Perhaps they [exhausted] the oyster beds that were easiest to get to, and clams were a fine alternative. In these middens, oyster shells are near the surface, but they're mostly pure clam."

Chicora chief Clyde Strickland speculated that some sort of red tide—an algae bloom that can kill fish and make shellfish toxic—made oysters unsafe to eat but didn't affect the clams. However, the reason for the abundance of clamshells and absence of oyster shells at the south end of the Grand Strand remains a mystery.

"It's sad that we don't know more about our Native American culture," Brockington said. "That loss of handing down from generation to generation—we would have known about the shell middens if [the Indians] hadn't been removed from their land."

In the spring and early summer, giant sturgeon averaging eight feet long and weighing three hundred pounds migrated from the ocean into the freshwater rivers to spawn and were an important food source since one fish could feed practically the entire village.

Chief Strickland said that the Chicora Indians even caught small whales. "They could get a whale if it came in close enough to the shoreline," he said. "They'd have fifteen to twenty-five people in canoes, five or six in each canoe with spears. If it was a gigantic whale, that's another story, but one about twice the size of a car would have been manageable." To harvest smaller fish, nets were used.

Chief Hatcher often demonstrates the old ways of trapping. The Waccamaw People used every part of an animal—boiling hooves for glue, using feathers on their arrows and saving eyeballs and intestines for fish bait or to bait a trap.

When asked how birds were caught, the Chief explained that sometimes arrows were used, but more often traps were utilized. A square hole about eighteen inches deep was dug, and then a few kernels of corn were placed in the hole. Birds landed to eat the corn with wings tucked in, but when they tried to fly back out, the dimensions of the hole prevented them from spreading their wings, and they were trapped. Another way to snare birds involved cutting a hole in a tree and inserting a stick. A loop of string was placed on the stick, along with a piece of corn. When the bird perched on the stick, it fell out of the tree, and the string tightened around the bird's legs.

Once local Indians became less nomadic, they had communal and individual gardens. A trinity of plants called Three Sisters was common throughout American tribes: climbing pole beans were planted around corn, and the corn stalks supported the bean vines. Squash was planted around the corn to keep weeds down.

The Horry County Museum in Conway has several artifacts demonstrating Native Americans' gardening and cooking methods. A thick digging stick about four feet long and sharpened at one end was used to poke holes in the ground and drop in seeds. Hoes were made with whelk shells bound to sticks.

A sort of mortar and pestle called a grinding stone was a large, flat rock paired with a smooth, round stone. The example at the museum has a worn

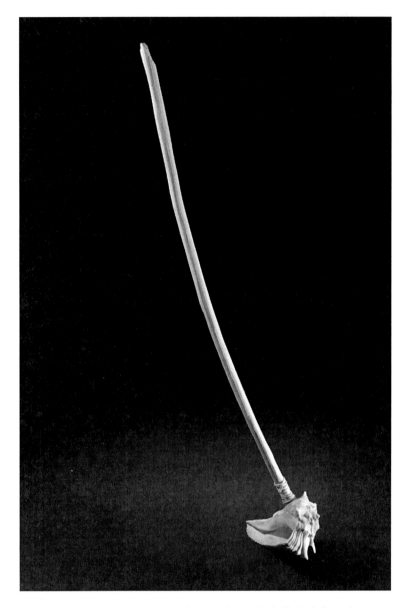

Native American garden hoes were fashioned out of whelk shells bound to sticks; this one is on display at the Horry County Museum in Conway. *Photo by Matt Silfer, Silfer Studios.*

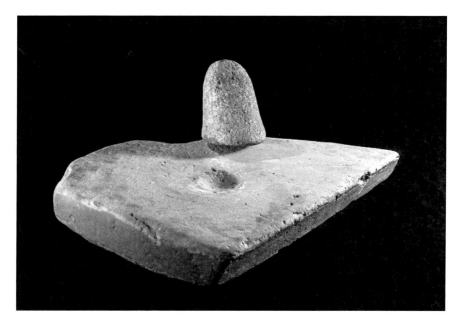

Native Americans ground grain by using a combination of round and flat stones. This set is on display at the Horry County Museum in Conway. *Photo by Matt Silfer, Silfer Studios.*

depression in the flat sandstone rock's middle where grains and other foods were ground fine enough to use in breads and gruels.

Corn, or maize, was an extremely important part of native diets. They ground it into meal to make a type of cornbread known as journeycakes, johnnycakes or hoecakes. They made balls of cornmeal dough and boiled them for early versions of hushpuppies. Indians made corn hominy—they made lye by soaking wood ash and then soaked corn in water with some of the lye added so the outer hull came off. Native Americans also parched and ground corn for an early version of grits. Corn was so important to Native Americans that throughout the Southeast, tribes celebrated its harvest with a Green Corn Ceremony.

Tubers such as sweet potatoes were also grown and stored in potato banks. The coastal climate and soil is perfect for growing the fall crop. Berries, nuts and herbs were gathered, and many accounts by early explorers and settlers describe local Indians as cultivating fruit orchards and nut tree groves.

The coast's humidity prevented much meat preservation. If meats weren't prepared fresh, sometimes small pieces were dried without a lot of salt or mixed with fats and grains for an early version of protein bars called pemmican, mainly to create food for journeys.

"We get our granola bars from pemmican," said Ben Abercrombie, director of Playcard Environmental Education Center in western Horry County. "It's like taking a Fruit Roll-Up and mixing it with meat. They'd take any kinds of meat scraps they had and mix it with fruits and jellies and mash it down and dry it in the sun, then roll it up in leaves like a big leathery Fruit Roll-Up. That would be their hunting party snack."

When fresh meals were cooked, Chief Hatcher said, meats might be skewered and cooked by a fire. Another way to cook meats and vegetables was in clay pots. He said that flat-bottom pots could not withstand the heat of being suspended directly over the fire, so the Indians heated rocks and used sticks to drop them into the pots.

Chief Strickland added that clay pottery was created or "fired" in kilns that were dug into the ground. The pots were then used as cooking vessels in a similar manner by burying them in areas where the ground was heated near fires to make little baking chambers. Lips around some pots' top edges were where vines or sweetgrass ropes were looped so the pots could be cast into flowing waters and retrieved for water used in cooking or for drinking.

Tightly woven watertight sweetgrass baskets could also be used for cooking if they contained enough liquid to prevent scorching and were not placed directly over fires, Chief Strickland said, and such baskets were often used for soaking dried beans or holding foodstuffs.

Native Americans also had grills of a sort, Chief Strickland said. "They used limber tree limb branches that were still green with lots of moisture so they would not burn," he said. "They'd bend them over the fire and hang pots from them or use them as a grill like today's gas grill or charcoal grill. They'd make a rack with them."

Wild herbs were gathered to flavor the stews. Abercrombie said that one that flourishes like a weed in Horry County is a type of fennel. Chief Strickland noted that sage, spearmint and wild onions were also used, and apple wood was a favorite in cooking fires for infusing meats with its flavor.

This way of life began to change in the early sixteenth century.

INDIAN STEW

Second Chief Judicial Cheryl Sievers, the Waccamaw Indian People

1 cup flour
salt and pepper, to taste
½ teaspoon garlic powder
½ teaspoon onion powder
2¼ pounds venison roast, cubed
canola oil
1 sweet onion, chopped
2 cloves garlic, chopped
1 red bell pepper, chopped
2 stalks celery, chopped
8–10 red potatoes, parboiled and cubed
1 bag parsnips, parboiled and rough chopped
2 cubes beef bouillon
2 cups water
2 bay leaves

Mix together flour, salt, pepper, garlic powder and onion powder in a large bowl. Add venison cubes and toss to coat. Heat canola oil in a large skillet and brown the meat. Place browned meat in a slow cooker and add remaining ingredients; cook all day on low heat.
NOTE: Some people use rutabagas instead of parsnips. You can also add fresh harvest ingredients such as squash, sweet potatoes or corn. Beef can be substituted for the venison.

Chapter 2
EXPLORERS AND SETTLERS

Spanish explorers didn't leave behind their recipes, but they did help preserve the history of Grand Strand Indians and their culinary traditions.

In 1521, Captain Francisco Gordillo landed near Winyah Bay by present-day Georgetown. He didn't establish settlements, but he and his crew did kidnap several dozen Indians and enslave them, as described on the Waccamaw People's website, waccamaw.org.

One of those slaves was a young Indian boy they named Francisco de Chicora, who learned Spanish and used storytelling in a sort of Scheherazade manner that led to him making it all the way to Spain. The stories Francisco de Chicora told about his wonderful homeland piqued the Spaniards' interest in the New World.

Petyr Martyr d'Anghiera heard De Chicora's tales, and he published them in a 1530 chronicle titled *De Orbe Novo*, containing the story of "The Testimony of Francisco de Chicora." In that account, De Chicora described his tribe members as having domesticated deer herds for milk and cheese along with domesticated ducks, chickens, geese and other fowl. He mentioned that his people ate cornbread, a millet-type grain called xathi, potatoes, grapes and figs.

In 1526, Gordillo's superior and Francisco de Chicora's master, Lucas Vasquez de Ayllon, returned to the Winyah Bay area. Francisco de Chicora was brought along as a translator, but he escaped, and the Spaniards never saw him again.

The Spanish ships left for Central and South America, where stealing precious metals from the Incas and mining for gold and silver occupied them for many years. However, the Spaniards left behind diseases like smallpox, measles and influenza. Native Americans didn't have much resistance to them, and Indian populations began to diminish.

BRITISH INVASION

South Carolina Indians had several years of respite from Europeans after the Spaniards' 1526 visit. A group of French Huguenots attempted a settlement in 1562 in the Port Royal area, but it was abandoned in 1563. It wasn't until 1680 that the British made a settlement at Charles Towne.

In 1700, a Native American guide led John Lawson, a British naturalist, on a journey from Charles Towne to New Bern, North Carolina. During that trip, according to *Food in Colonial and Federal America* author Sandra L. Oliver, they ate many meals with Native Americans. Lawson documented eating roasted meat he called "barbakues" and noted that their pots were "continually boiling full of Meat, for Morning to night."

In 1732, British surveyors began to lay out Kingston Township along the banks of the Waccamaw River. The late Horry County historian Catherine Lewis wrote in *Horry County, South Carolina, 1730–1993* of a group of eager settlers visiting the site in 1734, where "they killed and barbecued a bear—the first recorded example of this fine old Horry tradition."

But even earlier than the official construction of Kingston Township, hardy British settlers had formed a loosely formed coastal fishing village called Little River, which still thrives near the North Carolina border. Records show British subjects settling there as early as 1734, lured by the promise of fifty acres of land apiece. Lewis described how in 1740 the Reverend George Whitefield visited Little River on New Year's Day and "found the inhabitants celebrating with fiddling and dancing."

This was a full century before stoves began to be used, so cooking was done in hearths using cast-iron pots, especially after the mid-1700s. Dutch ovens—named for a superior Dutch method of making the vessels copied by Englishman Abraham Darby—had handles and concave lids. The handles allowed the pots to be suspended over the fire, and the wells on the lids were designed for hot coals to be heaped on top, creating a miniature oven.

Another popular cast-iron cooking vessel was the "spider," which was like a Dutch oven with long legs that could be placed over a fire and also have coals heaped on its lid. Other models had short legs that could be placed directly over coals or be suspended; this way, when it was removed from the heat source, its bottom did not rest directly on the floor or table. Some pots had "ears" on the sides that metal-hinged pot hooks (they looked a little like ice block tongs) could grab onto so hot pots could be lifted safely.

So what did these early Horry County settlers put in those pots? Lewis wrote, "They did learn something of Indian foods and medicines, probably from remnants of the tribes who remained in the area."

New World and Old World recipes began to merge, with Indians showing settlers how to reap the bounty of their new homeland. Wild game, fresh and saltwater fish and seafood and vegetables hardy enough to grow in intense southern heat and coastal soil were consumed. Sausages were made as they had been in England, which Walter Hill noted was a type of "green sausage," more like what we would consider salami.

European colonists brought with them Irish (white) potatoes, tomatoes and chili peppers (which were brought to them from South and Central America by New World explorers) along with beef and dairy cattle, chickens and pigs.

Another Indian habit adopted out of necessity was using every bit of nourishment available, a trait already practiced by some of the settlers who brought with them recipes for dishes like headcheese, or souse. After butchering a hog, the head was boiled until the meat was tender; then it was finely diced, mixed with seasonings and cooled until it could be sliced and eaten.

Pork was smoked, hung and dried to prevent insects from laying eggs on the meat (and it added a tasty flavor). If the preservation process went wrong, the winter's meat supply was ruined. In those days, pigs were bred to have more fat than meat because lard was a valuable commodity. "They used lard for cooking to salves to greasing door hinges," Walter Hill said.

Corn, beans and squash—the Native Americans' Three Sisters—were embraced. Early settlers ate corn pone, cornbread, corn mush, corn porridge, roasted corn, corn fritters and hoecakes. On special occasions, they might make corn pudding.

Squash, sweet potatoes and pumpkins were baked and stewed and used in breads, pies and casseroles. Beans were standard side dishes but more often were incorporated into one-pot meals because most of these early settlers were not wealthy and didn't have more than a few cooking utensils. Wild game stews and fish chowders with vegetables and tubers were common.

Contact with Europeans was a death sentence for many Native Americans because they had little immunity against European diseases. In 1770, Lewis noted, William Bull II wrote in a letter to the Earl of Hillsboro, "I cannot quit the Indians without mentioning an observation that has often raised my wonder. That in this Province, settled in 1670…Then swarming with tribes of Indians, there remain now, except the few Catawbas, nothing of them but their names, within three hundred miles of our seacoast."

Some estimates say as many as 90 percent of American Indians died from European diseases. Others died in conflicts with settlers, British and French troops and different tribes or were simply forced off their land by white settlers.

Eliza Lucas Pinckney of the Georgetown and Charleston County areas wrote in a 1761 letter to her business agent in England, George Morley, "I know not what to tell you of our affairs in the Indian Country on wch. to found any real satisfaction our army are still there, we have destroy'd Sevl. of their Towns, but when you consider what Indian Towns are, and how soon rebuilt, you will think we need not be too much elated with the success we have had hithertoo unless we had killed more Indians. this is certain we know but of two that have been yet killd though they tell us sevl are missing."

The reason present-day Native Americans whose ancestors lived in the Grand Strand area don't know more of their own history is because they were removed from their land. "A people loses its culture when it loses its land," historian Lee Brockington said. "So when Native Americans were driven off their land, they began to lose a great deal of their culture compared to more of our Lowcountry and slave laborers who were emancipated but often stayed on the land."

EUROPEAN IMMIGRANTS

While the majority of early Grand Strand settlers were from England, other nationalities also made homes here.

Some Dutch settlers came here in 1671. French Huguenots who escaped religious persecution in their homeland made their way up from Charles Towne beginning around 1690. A larger contingent of Scotch moved down from North Carolina beginning in 1682, and Germans arrived in the 1700s. According to *Horry County, South Carolina: 1730–1993*, John Vaught, whose descendants still live in the area, emigrated from Germany and settled in the Little River area.

Today many Vereens descended from the French Huguenots make their homes throughout the Grand Strand. Russell Vereen, owner of Russell's

Seafood Grill & Raw Bar in Murrells Inlet, and his father, Sam Vereen, can trace their roots back to the first Vereens (aka Varin—the spelling was changed in the early 1700s) who came to South Carolina in the mid-1600s. One of those ancestors, Jacques Varin (1650–1699), married Susanne Horry (1655–1725). Horry is another venerable French Huguenot name throughout the Grand Strand area, and Horry County is named for one of that family's descendants: Revolutionary War hero Peter Horry.

Elizabeth "Bessie" Waties Allston Pringle of Georgetown County (1845–1921) wrote of her great-grandfather, Jean Louis Gibert, who brought one of the last groups of Huguenots in 1764 and settled "some 300 miles into the interior of [South Carolina] where their grant was…and they set to work to clear land and plant the cuttings of grape-vines to make wine." Just nine years later, Gibert's love of fine foods caused his demise. Gibert had brought with him from France

> a devoted and capable attendant, Pierre Le Roy, who in this wilderness filled many and diverse offices; he delighted to vary the often very limited diet of the pasteur by preparing for him dainty dishes of mushrooms with which he was familiar in the old country. There are many varieties here unknown there, and any one who knows this delicious but dangerous vegetable, knows how easily confounded are the good and the poisonous; the deadly Aminita resembles very closely one of the best edible mushrooms; we know not exactly how, but one night the dainty dish proved fatal to the great and good pasteur.

Many settlers came to South Carolina through indentured servitude, according to Sandra Oliver's *Food in Colonial and Federal America*:

> Many young people immigrated to America, most of them going to labor-starved Virginia and Maryland in the seventeenth and early eighteenth centuries, having agreed to a period of voluntary servitude, called an indenture, in exchange for the cost of their transportation to the colonies, living expenses, and other immigration costs. At the end of the indenture, usually lasting between four and seven years—during which they usually lived with their master's family, sharing bed and board—they received a sum of money, or occasionally land, and new clothing. They were free to marry, have a family, and establish their own farm or trade. In the Carolinas, about a third of the settlers began as indentured servants who gained 100 acres from the proprietors upon freedom; many acquired additional land afterward.

All of these immigrants brought recipes from their homelands. From England came a fondness of "meat, bread and ale," Oliver wrote. The Dutch also enjoyed bread and meat and added a fondness for fresh, salted and dried fish. Holland was known for its sugar refineries, which was reflected in Dutch colonists' baking.

UNWILLING AND UNWITTING IMMIGRANTS

Also in the mid-1600s, black slaves began to be brought to South Carolina from the Caribbean, mostly by English slavers who brought African slaves to the West Indies.

In about 1700, colonists in the Charles Towne area figured out that rice would grow well along the southern Carolina coast. About the same time, they discovered that natives of West Africa were experts at growing coastal rice using a tidal flow method. After this, the slave trade didn't just boom—it exploded.

It's estimated that between 10 and 20 million slaves were brought to the United States and that more than 40 percent of all African slaves brought to America before the Revolutionary War arrived at Charles Towne. By 1720, there were twice as many black slaves as whites in South Carolina, and in 1740, the state's population was 90 percent black.

Slaves were often purchased from African kings—sometimes through barter—and as many as six hundred kidnapped Africans at a time were packed into ships like cordwood for a journey across the Atlantic Ocean referred to as the Middle Passage. They were fed and cared for poorly during the voyage to America—sometimes fed only raw peanuts and corn—and the deaths of up to 20 percent of each group were considered the "normal price of doing business," according to South Carolina's Information Highway (SCIWAY).

One slave merchant, John Barbot, is cited in a paper titled "African Crops and Slave Cuisine" by Joseph E. Holloway, PhD, as noting that "a ship that takes in 500 slaves, must provide above 100,000 yams," which translates into two hundred yams per person. Holloway quoted a slave recently arrived from Africa who told a free black in Charleston what he ate on the ship: "We had nothing to eat but yams, which were thrown amongst us at random—and of those we had scarcely enough to support life. More than a third of us died on the passage, and when we arrived at Charleston, I was not able to stand."

The African yams on the slave ships were not the same as American sweet potatoes. Although they are similar, yams are starchier and usually larger, and when they're cooked, yams are not as creamy as sweet potatoes. However, some people in the Grand Strand say "yams" when they're actually cooking with sweet potatoes.

Holloway said that other foods fed to slaves on various ships included plantain, cornbread, fish, rice, limes, peppers, palm oil and field peas. To keep their valuable investments happy, slave owners allowed many traditional African and Caribbean foods to become part of slaves' diets, especially grown in the slaves' gardens. Encouraging slaves to grow their own food also saved the masters money.

Although some sources on American slave foods note that many of the African foods introduced by slaves to South Carolina foodways came with them on slave ships, Sandra Oliver pointed out that is not a practical theory, citing a 1774 letter from John Adams to Abigail Adams:

> *While there are some claims that slaves "brought" seeds or certain foodstuffs with them, the circumstances of their unplanned, forced emigration worked against their being prepared to bring favorite food seeds or plants with them. Some slave merchants and shippers, however, observed the slaves' refusal to eat unfamiliar food, and soon comprehended the necessity of providing familiar fare to feed slaves en route to America or the West Indies.*
>
> *In addition, enslaved blacks working as sailors, translators, and body servants traveled with their white owners to and from Africa and other places. These people were culture bearers, often trading and bartering with the urban slaves with whom they had contact. These slaves had an opportunity to procure familiar and desired foods—okra, sesame, black-eyed peas, hyacinth beans, pigeon peas, and eggplants—and introduce them into the colonies.*

Chapter 3
RICE PLANTATIONS

I n the span of a few decades, rice became a vastly significant part of the local economy and made fortunes for several dozens of plantation owners. The first seed grains came into the port of Charles Towne in the late seventeenth century, and it didn't take long for farmers to realize that the freshwater tidal areas of Georgetown County were ideal for rice production. By 1691, rice production was already so firmly established that the South Carolina General Assembly voted to allow residents to pay their taxes in rice.

At first, rice was grown in upland areas, but the new rice farmers realized that natives of West Africa's "Rice Coast," which had a climate similar to coastal South Carolina, knew

This rice winnowing basket at the Horry County Museum was used to shake and toss rice in the air; the wind would blow away the chaff. *Photo by Matt Silfer, Silfer Studios.*

how to make their businesses grow. That's when slave importation took off, and in only about fifty years, the slaves outnumbered whites by nine to one.

Slave labor was vital to the plantations' success. By the mid-eighteenth century, an extremely labor-intensive rice-growing method called the tidal flow system had been implemented. Slaves dug hundreds of miles of canals that carried fresh water to the fields for necessary floodings. They built wood trunks (huge valves) that controlled the flow. Once the infrastructure was in place, the growing process entailed grueling labor in extreme heat and muddy, mucky, mosquito-infested conditions.

After trial and error to see which types of rice grew best along the South Carolina coast, a variety that became internationally prized was named Carolina Gold Rice. It has a slight golden hue and a tantalizing aroma and flavor.

Field Hands

Weak, dazed and confused slaves were put to work right away on rice plantations such as those in Georgetown County.

In the early eighteenth century, according to SCIWAY, slaves were often housed in

> *minimal huts built of upright poles set in a trench and covered in clay. The roofs were probably covered in palmetto fronds or other thatch. Archaeologists called these houses "wall-trench structures" and they were used at least up to the American Revolution. Most had no fireplaces and they were built with earthen floors. The buildings range from about 13 feet in length and only 9 feet in width up to about 21 feet in length and around 14 feet in width. There were only a few windows and these were all open, with perhaps only a shutter to close out the bad weather.*

Gradually, their dwellings evolved to include fireplaces and then, in the 1800s, further changed to become the conventional rows of wood-frame structures typically thought of as slave cabins.

Bessie Pringle described mid-nineteenth-century slave quarters at Georgetown County's Chicora Wood Plantation: "The houses were built regularly about fifty yards apart on each side of a wide road, with fruit-trees

This circa 1905 photo shows a former slave cabin and seven African American occupants at Hobcaw Barony's Friendfield Village. Built of heart pine lumber on brick pilings, the chimney is made of brick and tabby—a type of concrete/mortar made with oyster shells. It was enlarged to include two rear rooms and a front porch. Note the fishing net and sharpening stone. *Belle W. Baruch Collection, Belle W. Baruch Foundation and Georgetown County Library, Georgetown, South Carolina.*

on each side. There are generally about twelve houses on each side, so that it makes a little village." Chicora Wood had three such villages.

The slaves cooked outside over open hearths or, later, inside at their fireplaces, which usually necessitated cooking meals in one pot that slow-cooked all day while they worked in the fields. SCIWAY notes that there is little evidence that early slaves had eating utensils, meaning they likely ate with their fingers. In later years, there is evidence of wooden spoons, mollusk shells and broken pottery used as eating utensils. The pots were stirred with wooden paddles or spoons.

Having two meals per day was common for many slaves, although three was typical for others. Sometimes slave cooks received rations for all the plantations' slaves and doled them out mess hall style either near the fields or in communal dining halls. Other slaves cooked their own breakfasts and suppers and ate meals at their cabins.

Master-supplied food rations were based on how much work each slave performed, with women receiving less than men and children getting "about half the rations as adult hands." Rations varied from plantation to plantation, but a typical allotment described in *What the Slaves Ate: Recollections of African American Foods and Foodways* by Herbert C. Covey and Wight Eisnach included, "for an adult, a daily quart of cornmeal and one-half pound of salt pork, which were supplemented by an occasional sweet potato, peas, rice, and fruit. Many historians have reported that slaves received about three pounds of boneless pork per week."

Charles Joyner, author of *Down by the Riverside*, provided much insight into eighteenth- and nineteenth-century rice plantation slaves' diets in the All Saints Parish area, which spanned Horry and Georgetown Counties. "The slaves' rations were usually distributed on Saturday afternoons and had to last until the following Saturday, supplemented by food from the slaves' gardens and animals they raised. If the allowance ran out before the end of the week, as it did on some plantations, the slaves had to steal or do without." Dirleton and Birdfield Plantation owner James Ritchie Sparkman doled out weekly rations

> *of Meal 10 quarts, of Rice or Peas 8 quarts, and of Sweet Potatoes one Bushel. This is the full allowance of every adult, and the younger negroes the same, no matter what their age, as soon as they are put to task work. Molasses is given throughout the year at proper intervals. Salt Fish only in winter, Pork or Bacon and Beef during summer. The allowance of Molasses is 1 pint (for one week), of Salted Fish (Mullet or Mackerel) 2 or 3 according to size, of Pork or Bacon 2 lbs.*

From June through November, Joyner documented, Sparkman's slaves also received daily allowances of two quarts of beef and rice soup.

Colonel Peter Horry, a Revolutionary War hero who fought with General Francis "Swamp Fox" Marion and for whom Horry County is named, had four plantations in the Georgetown area. Coastal Carolina University history professor Roy Talbert Jr., in a 1998 CCU Distinguished Teacher-Scholar Lecturer Series called "So Fine a Beach: Peter Horry's Summer of 1812," wrote that the colonel personally distributed food allowances of "a peck of corn a week, plus small amounts of whatever garden produce, such as potatoes, was in season. Christmas was an exception, when Horry gave his slaves rice and a bull to slaughter. Once, when he had a crew of slaves raising a new house, he rewarded them with rice, bacon and whiskey."

So, food rations varied from plantation to plantation, and sometimes they were particularly meager. Charles Joyner wrote of an account from Caroline

Small, the daughter of Titus and Silvey Small. They were the slaves of John D. Magill at Richmond Hill Plantation, who was notoriously harsh. At Richmond Hill, "a week's food for a slave family was a peck of sweet potatoes, a dozen salted fish; if there was a baby in the family you got one peck of grits and one piece of fat back. In the summertime you got one peck of meal and one quart of syrup."

The meal was cornmeal, and cornbread was the field slaves' most common bread. There were many ways to make cornbread—the Indians' method of mixing meal and water and rolling it in leaves or corn husks to bake in ashes near a fire or perhaps baking it in cast-iron pots with coals heaped on the lids.

They also ate poor cuts of meat their masters didn't want such as pigs' heads, feet and entrails. It is from these days that chitterlings (intestines) and maw (the stomach, or tripe) became part of slaves' diets. Joyner wrote, "Hog-butchering time meant spare ribs, bacon, and chitterlings for the slaves, the other parts being reserved for the master." Especially in the latter years of slavery, some slaves raised their own pigs and cows and sold extras to their masters. Chickens were kept for eggs, and on special occasions, they were slaughtered and fried or put into a pot with rice for pilau.

Usually, slaves were allowed to have their own vegetable gardens, and plant-based foods made up much of their diets. Slaves' vegetable gardens, whether communal or individual, were tended on days off and after their days' allotted work, or tasks, were finished. They raised corn, sweet potatoes, white potatoes, tomatoes, collards, turnips, peanuts, okra, eggplant, beans and peas, according to Joyner. Peas could mean green peas, but more likely it refers to field peas or cowpeas.

Field peas and rice, known today as a dish called Hoppin' John, would have been familiar to Africans accustomed to the same sort of dish in their homelands. Cooking was a way they could stay connected to their culinary roots, and the slaves' unique ways of preparing and flavoring foods introduced another style into Grand Strand culinary history.

American Indians were also enslaved on rice plantations, although not nearly in the same vast numbers as African slaves. But their knowledge of what foods grow well along the coastal areas, as well as what types of foods were available for foraging, aided and influenced fellow slaves' and their masters' diets.

In *The Carolina Housewife* by Charlestonian Sarah Rutledge, first published in 1847, she included a recipe for Seminole Soup: "Take a squirrel, cut it up and put it on to boil. When the soup is nearly done add to it one pint of picked hickory-nuts and a spoonful of parched and powdered sassafras leaves—or the tender top of a pine tree, which gives a very aromatic flavor to the soup."

Rutledge also had a recipe for Chicora cornbread: "To one quart of milk, add six eggs well beaten, one table-spoonful of wheat flour, one tea-spoonful of salaeratus, a large table-spoonful of butter, one table-spoonful of brown sugar, with as much corn meal as will make a thick batter; add a little salt, and bake, as soon as mixed, in tin or earthen pans."

Although plantation owners had orchards, slaves gathered fruit in the wild, like berries, or grew fruit in their gardens, such as watermelons and pumpkins. They also cultivated fig trees and scuppernong grapes. Joyner wrote that sometimes plantation owners could buy inexpensive imported Caribbean fruit from ships sailing the Waccamaw.

Slaves fished fresh and salt water for sturgeon, shad, mullet, perch, pike, spot, bream and more to supplement their meat supply, along with seafood like crabs, oysters, shrimp and clams. They used nets, traps, baited lines, gigs, poles and wooden rakes to gather their harvests.

Opossums were easy to catch and frequently made their way into stew pots. Freshwater terrapin turtles were eaten, and marine loggerhead turtles and their eggs were special treats. Some slaves were allowed to use guns for hunting, and they sought raccoons, squirrels, deer, rabbits, alligator, bear and many types of fowl, including blackbirds, geese, ducks and wild turkeys.

Ricebirds, or bobolinks, were the bane of plantation owners because they descended en masse to strip away rice grains. However, they were good eating, although it took several of the tiny birds to make a meal for one person.

Louisa Brown was a former slave born in 1857 who was interviewed in the 1930s by Genevieve W. Chandler of Murrells Inlet as part of the Works Progress Administration's Federal Writers' Project. Brown said that weddings were times of feasts on her plantation. "We marry to Turkey Hill Plantation," Brown remembered of her own wedding. "Hot supper. Cake, wine, and all. Kill cow, hog, chicken and all. That time when you marry, so much to eat!"

But when Charles Joyner interviewed Brown's daughter, Mary Small, in the 1970s, she "reported that her mother told her many a meal consisted of nothing more than corn meal mush and molasses in a pan."

Sundays could include special treats. At Chicora Wood Plantation, Adele Petigru Allston (1810–1896) held catechism for slave children. "After the lesson," wrote Allston's daughter, Bessie Pringle, "a big cake was brought in a wheelbarrow by one of the house-boys, convoyed by Maum Mary, who cut it with much ceremony, and each child went up to the barrow, dropped a courtesy and received a slice, then passed to my mother with another courtesy, filed out and scampered happily home as soon as safe from Maum Mary's paralyzing eye."

DINING AT THE BIG HOUSE

Provisions were better for slaves who worked in their masters' grand plantation houses. They "often ate the same food as the master's family," Joyner wrote, "and they usually ate in the kitchen either before or after the master's family was served."

Wealthy rice plantation owners dined well. Their cooks, who were slaves, put African flavors and recipes into the menus, as well as learned their masters' and mistresses' recipes. When it was required for a slave cook to learn a new recipe, it was read to him or her until it was memorized.

"Breakfast, served anytime between 7 and 9 a.m., was a light meal for the planter's family and the house servants," Joyner wrote. "Wyndham Malet wrote of breakfasting on stewed peaches, bread, and clabber." Clabber is soured milk left out overnight to solidify into a spongy jell, and in those days, it was considered a delicacy. Walter Hill said that his research shows that the whey was strained off the clabber to leave a rich and creamy product similar to crème fraîche.

Bessie Pringle described a typical breakfast as "hominy and butter, and an egg or a piece of sausage and then a waffle and syrup or honey."

"Dinner, the midday meal, constituted 'the great business of the day,'" Joyner wrote. "Dining around 2 p.m., the lowcountry gentry—and their servants—might enjoy a variety of meats (ham, mutton, venison, turkey, oysters, and turtle in combination were not uncommon) topped off by desserts (assorted puddings and pies), wines, and cordials."

Eliza Lucas Pinckney (1722–1793), daughter of George Lucas and Anne Mildrum, grew up in Antigua, where her father was a second-generation Antiguan and the island's lieutenant governor. In 1739, her family moved to South Carolina, where her grandfather, John Lucas, had rice plantations. She spent several years at school in England.

As a teenager, Eliza acted as her father's plantation manager at Wappoe, with "twenty working Slaves," as chronicled in the Papers of Eliza Lucas

Pinckney and Harriott Pinckney Horry (digital edition) and collected by the University of Virginia Press, and she is credited as a talented and inquisitive agriculturalist who established a profitable indigo crop and later experimented with cultivating mulberry trees "in an attempt to develop an American silk industry."

She married Charles Pinckney in 1744, and the plantation she supervised was lost to her father's creditors. However, the indigo crop she started turned a profit in 1745. Over the course of the next fifteen or so years, Eliza lived in England but moved back to South Carolina again in 1758. Charles contracted malaria and died, and Eliza became widowed at age thirty-six. She moved to her husband's Belmont Plantation in Orangeburg County.

As a mature housewife, Eliza wrote down 104 recipes in a booklet that are included in the University of Virginia Press's digital archives as edited versions of an out-of-print 1956 publication of Eliza's receipt book. Several recipes are homeopathic medical cures, such as using oil of amber mixed with sugar to cure "the Hiccough" or using wormwood "For ye Gout." On the culinary side, she recorded how to make gooseberry vinegar, teacakes, marmalades, pudding, roast beef (that recipe's name is "To Dobe a Rump of Beef") and a spicy condiment called "Queen Sauce."

Until her death in 1793, Eliza's documents and correspondence provide a fascinating record of not only what the elite people of her time ate but also of the area's culinary customs and gardens. She is a valuable link between European and Caribbean colonists and their influence on Grand Strand dining customs, as she lived with and influenced the dining habits of her daughter, Harriott Pinckney Horry (1748–1830), who lived a little south of Georgetown near present-day McClellanville at Hampton Plantation.

Many of the recipes use humble ingredients, such as one for "A Common Bread Pudding" using bread, eggs, milk and sugar, although the lemon peel called for at the end was probably not a handy ingredient for most rural colonists. All of the recipes provide fascinating glimpses into colonial lives, since little is more intimate than what people choose to cook and eat.

Eliza made an old English dish, Caveach, which she titled "To Pickle Mackerel Calld Ceveechd." It calls for poking holes in mackerel pieces, inserting seasonings and browning them in oil before marinating them in spiced vinegar. In her recipe for preserving whole apricots, we're reminded that it was English colonists who brought that fruit to the East Coast. Thomas Jefferson raised artichokes at Monticello in the 1760s, and Eliza, the enthusiastic gardener, must also have grown them because she noted how to bury them layered with sand to "keep artichoaks all the year."

Hampton Plantation, located south of Georgetown, was built in the early eighteenth century and is a state historic site open for public tours. *Author's collection.*

Eliza either cultivated a peach orchard or had access to one because she wrote of pickling them and making peach brandy called Ratifie that utilized six hundred peach pits. She coagulated milk with rennet (Eliza spelled it "runnet") she made herself and preserved hams in a German style (the receipt is called "To make Westphalian Hamms") by laying them in salt for a week to ten days and then in a brine for three weeks made from a mixture of boiled brown sugar, salt, saltpeter and water before hanging and smoking them. In other recipes, Eliza gave specific instructions about what type of cookware to use. Pears must be baked in pewter, she noted, while apples should be baked in a "mazarine dish," which is a type of metal strainer.

We're also reminded of some of the less delicious aspects of colonial cookery, such as in Eliza's advice "To Recover Veal when it has grown Sower," which is to "rub it over with Vinegar just before you lay it to the fire and as well as you can between the joynts." Another recipe for pickling hams and tongues suggests smoking them with "horse litter."

Some gleanings of the local cuisine of the mid-eighteenth century are found in preserved letters Eliza wrote. In a letter dated May 2, 1740, she wrote to a friend in England, Mary Steer (Mrs. Richard) Boddicott, and said,

"This Country is in General fertile and abounds with Venison and wild fowl; the Venison is much higher flavoured than in England but 'tis seldom fatt."

In a letter dated June 4, 1741 (three years before she was married), to her father, who was in Antigua, Eliza said that she was going to send him requested provisions of a barrel of butter, corn and ginger. She mentioned ginger in another letter, and it seems that she grew a great quantity of it. The teenager was performing admirably as a plantation manager, since a letter dated November 11, 1741, indicated that she had supplies to spare to send to William Murray in the West Indies. He was the recipient of "a boat load of white oak Staves bacon and salted beef for the West Indias. Sent up at the same time a barl. salt ½ salt peter some brown Sugar for the bacon and 6 sugar and a couple bottles rum for Mrs. Murry. And desire he will send down all the butter and hogs lard." Still, there are some items Eliza couldn't or didn't easily grow. In a 1741 letter, she thanked her cousin in Boston, Fanny Fayerweather, for a gift of apples.

We learn more about foods available at the time in a May 22, 1742 letter to her brother, Thomas, that describes where she is living:

> It abounds with fine navigable rivers, and great quantities of fine timber the Country at a great distance that is to say about a hundred or a hundred and fifty mile from Crs. Town very hilly, the Soil in general very fertile, and there is very few European or American fruits or grain but what grow here, The Country abounds with wild fowl Venison and fish Beef, veal and motton are here in much greater perfection than in the Islands, tho' not equal to that in England are but their pork exceeds any I ever tasted any where The Turkeys extreamly fine expecially the wild, and indeed all their poultry is exceedingly good. and peaches Nectrons and mellons of all sorts extreamly fine and in profusion and their Oranges exceed any I ever tasted in the West Indies or from spain or portugal.
>
> The people in genl hospitable and honest and the better sort add to these a polite gentile behavior. The poorer sort are the most indolent people in the world or they could never be wretched in so plentiful a country as this. The winters here are very fine and pleasant but 4 months in the year is extreamly disagreeable, excessive hott much thunder and lightening, and muskatoes and sand flies in abundance.
>
> The staple comodity here is rice and the only thing they export to Europe. beef pork and lumber they send to the west Indias.

In a September 8, 1742 letter to her father, Eliza noted that she ordered cucumber seed from West India. Another letter dated 1742 to her friend,

In this 1930s photograph, an unidentified woman and child on Sandy Island near Georgetown pound rice with a mortar and pestle, which was done to break and remove the hard outer covering of the rice. *Photo by Bayard Wootten. Brookgreen Gardens Collection, Georgetown County Library, Georgetown, South Carolina.*

Mary Bartlett, describes how she fills her days, which includes making a shrimp net and planting "a large figg orchard with design to dry and export them." She also noted that "I own I love the vegitable world extreamly I think it an innocent and useful amusement."

A postscript on the letter to Mary Bartlett gives an indication of how turtle was flavored: "Mama begs Mrs. Pinckneys acceptance of a little Indigo Seed, sorrel and negroe pepper the last a good Ingredient in dressing Turtle." "Negro pepper" refers to the seeds of a shrubby African tree with a flavor like black pepper mixed with nutmeg.

More of Eliza's preserved correspondence includes thanking her father in 1744 for sending sugar from Antigua because "what we have now in town is bad and dear and if it will not be intruding too much I shall be obliged to you for some white powdered sugar a thing that cant be purchased here at this time." In 1758, she sent a barrel of rice to her sons' school in England, noting, "The children love it boiled dry to eat with their meat instead of bread."

An invitation dated to about 1766 asks her to a party at the home of South Carolina governor Charles Montague to "eat a Barbecue Hog," and an undated letter makes reference to her slave Mary-Ann, "roasting poultry in the greatest perfection you ever saw," as well as enjoying Mary-Ann's pickled oysters.

About thirty years after Eliza began writing down her recipes, her daughter, Harriott Pinckney Horry, started recording her own recipes and included twenty-six of her mother's. Harriott was the mistress of Hampton Plantation, located just barely south of the boundary between Georgetown and Charleston Counties. It is one of several plantations encompassing six thousand acres along the Santee River owned by Daniel Horry. In the 1790 census, Hampton Plantation had 340 slaves listed.

In Harriott Pinckney Horry's cookbook, we get a glimpse of how the upper class of the time dined and of European and African influences in their cooking. Harriott was extremely well connected to the world's elite: President George Washington dined at Hampton Plantation in 1791; she visited the Dowager Princess Augusta at Kew in England as a child in 1753; she was connected by marriage to the Marquis de Lafayette; she visited Martha Custis Washington at Mount Vernon in 1793; and in 1807, she had her sweet potatoes sent to French empress Josephine Bonaparte.

Many of Harriott's recipes are rather complicated, and no doubt most of the hard labor of making them fell to her slaves, although there is evidence that she enjoyed cooking. At a time when all but the wealthiest citizens were lucky if they could afford a milk cow or two, Harriott made potted beef, ragout of veal breast and beef collops, which were thin beef strips in mushroom gravy. A fricassee of chicken contains more ingredients than most Grand Stranders of the day would have had handy, like anchovies, shallots, white wine and capers. A gourmet touch any present-day chef would appreciate is a recipe for raspberry vinegar.

In "To Dress a Calves Head," instructions involve many steps and ingredients, starting with boiling the head "till the Tongue will Peal" and ending with making "little Cakes of the Brains and dip them in and fry them," before the head is plated with oysters, brain patties, the tongue, bacon and forcemeat, garnished with horseradish and barberries. Another calf's head recipe called "To Dress a Calves head in imitation of Turtle" is a soup containing chicken in addition to the calf's head.

Her family ate muskmelons, mushroom "catchup," walnut catchup, stewed pigeons, quince marmalade and several different types of breads and cakes, including rice bread and Portugal cakes flavored with mace and rose water. The era's affinity for pudding (sometimes spelled "puding," with one *d*) is evident with many recipes, including apple pudding, carrot pudding, yam pudding, orange pudding and blancmange.

However, Harriott's household suffered privation during the American Revolution. Soldiers raided her gardens and stores, and she and her husband provided supplies for Patriot troops for which they were not compensated until after the war was over. Hooker wrote that at one point, twenty-six friends who fled Charles Towne's British occupation stayed with her.

During a 1793 trip to New England, Harriott kept detailed notes, and we get to see her shopping lists. She bought sheep, a shoat, chickens, turkeys, geese, ducks, a goat, hams, tongues, smoked beef, pickled pork, vinegar, live mint plants, parsley, capers, mustards, bottled honey, coffee, flour, butter, lard, pickled peppers, mangoes, onions, cheeses, rice, potatoes, sugar, eggs, sugar loaves, limes, apples, oranges, pounded ginger, cinnamon water, mint water and more.

In 1815, Harriott took another trip up north, and in Havre de Grace, Maryland, she tasted a white perch she described as having an "indifferent" taste, saying that it was "something in taste like our Doctor fish." On the same trip while at Lake George in New York State, she commented, "The water is uncommonly clear and a good deal of fish is caught particularly Salmon, trout Bass &c., but I have tasted none to equal our Santee fish."

The wealthy enjoyed what Richard Hooker described as "immensely" popular rum punch, as well as imported beverages such as wines, brandies, cider and teas. Harriott listed in her cookbook recipes for rum punch, cherry brandy, raspberry brandy, spruce beer and plumb brandy, and she also purchased wine, porter, brandy, rum and gin.

During the 1815 journey, Harriott saw an icebox (she called it a refrigerator) for the first time during a visit to Richmond, Virginia. She was fascinated by the device and described its appearance in detail, even drawing a sketch of its workings in her travel journal. During the same trip, while at Gadsby's Hotel in Baltimore, she was impressed by the "patent oven" and "a number of stoves set in brick work."

Yam Puding

From the Recipe Book of Eliza Lucas Pinckney *(1756)*

> *Take a pound of Yams boil'd dry, beat it fine in a Mortar with a pound Butter till it Puffs, take ten Eggs half the white, beat them with a pound of Sugar, add half a pint of wine with Spice, the Juice of a Lemon with a little of the rine, and some slices of Citron laid on the Top.*

To Boil Rice

From the Recipe Book of Eliza Lucas Pinckney *(1756)*

> *Take a pint of rice well picked and Clean'd set on a saucepann with one Gallon of water and a handful of salt when the water boils put in the rice about a quarter of an hour will boil it enough according to the quickness of the fire or by tasting it; but be sure to avoid stiring the rice after 'tis in the sauce-pann for one turn with a spoon will spoil all when 'tis tender turn the rice into a sieve; when the water is quite draind off return it in to the sauce pann and let it stand near the fire for an hour or more to be kept hott if the process is well observd it will be white, dry, and every grain separate.*
> [Eliza noted that the recipe came from "Mrs. Blakewey."]

STEW'D DUCKS

From A Colonial Plantation Cookbook: The Receipt Book of Harriott Pinckney Horry, 1770

> *Take a Duck (either wild or tame) split it down the back, make some Stuffing with Stale bread, the Liver of the duck, Spice, Parsley, Marjoram, Onion, Butter, Pepper and Salt, all chop'd up together, fill the duck with it and sew up the back, and put it into a Pott with Water enough to cover it let it stew till the Water is almost stew'd away then add a little Wine and a lump of Butter to the little that remains which makes the gravy and browns the Duck.*

RICE BREAD

From A Colonial Plantation Cookbook: The Receipt Book of Harriott Pinckney Horry, 1770

> *Take 4 quarts of rice beat it into flour, sift it, take one quart of the* [word illegible] *siftings and boil it soft, spread it in your tray and while just warm put in your leaven or yeast and mix by degrees all the flour in, put it to rise and when risen which will be seen by its cracking put it into your pans and bake it. NB. It will be so soft when put in the pans that you may dip it up.* [Harriott noted that the recipe came from "Mrs. McPherson."]

Chapter 4
EARLY MIDDLE-CLASS FOODS

Poor whites and slaves living in Horry and Georgetown Counties in colonial and antebellum periods drank water, Richard Hooker wrote, while the "average South Carolinian more likely drank a mixture of rum and water, spruce beer, or cider, and in frontier areas peach brandy and, increasingly, whiskey as well."

Not all slaves lived on rice plantations. Some middle-class citizens had slaves, and often one of them cooked for their owners. They would eat largely the same foods, "although not at the same table," according to Sandra Oliver.

As for their food sources, most poor and middle-class whites living throughout the Grand Strand had gardens, hunted and fished. They ate pole beans, squash, greens, pumpkins, sweet potatoes, Irish potatoes and corn in many variations, from grits to cornbread. However, they did not have roasted sweet corn. "We ate field corn," said Levon Hucks, who lives in western Horry County and whose family has lived in the area for many generations. "I didn't know what sweet corn was until I went to college."

Easy access to rice depended on proximity for someone living near the plantations or the rivers where foodstuffs were shipped. Some families regularly ate rice, many two or three times per day. Others, especially in outlying areas of Horry County, liked rice but could only afford to eat it on Sundays or at other special meals. In both cases, what the locals usually ate was "middlins," or broken rice. Whole grains were normally reserved for export or the wealthy elite.

Of course, all classes ate some of the same foods, and there were crossovers in preparation methods. But cooks in wealthy homes could afford fancier ingredients and more exotic flavorings to create dishes out of reach for common folks. For example, all classes ate turtle soup, which was also called cooter soup. "Cooter" is derived from the Bambara and Malinke word for turtle, which is *kuta*. The freshwater variety of turtles, or terrapins, were eaten by those living near rivers, while on the coast, seafaring loggerhead turtles provided a lot of meat, and their leathery-shelled eggs were also consumed.

But some recipes and preparation methods were different among the classes, too. Those with ordinary farm ingredients might put onions, potatoes and hardboiled eggs in the soup pot. People with more money and means could add sherry, Madeira, celery, cayenne pepper or lemon juice. Some foodstuffs that poor and middle-class residents could not grow or produce, like tea, coffee or refined sugar, were either purchased or done without.

As noted by Mary Tolford Wilson in her essay at the beginning of *The First American Cookbook*, published in 1796 by Amelia Simmons, European terms during this period slowly gave way to American culinary names, such as saying "molasses" instead of the British "treacle" and "cookie" or "cooky" in place of the Dutch term "koekje." Another Dutch food, "sla," which was salad, became "slaw" in America.

GULLAH GEECHEE CUISINE

Gullah Geechee culture, often referred to as just one or the other, came about when black slaves on the Sea Islands off South Carolina, Florida and Georgia developed a pidgin language that mixed various African languages with English and Caribbean dialects. The culture was insulated on the Sea Islands due to their remoteness.

This pidgin evolved into a new "auxiliary language" that allowed slaves from different countries to communicate with one another. Over time, overseers and plantation owners learned the pidgin, as well as plantation owners' children, who were nursed by slaves and played with slaves.

The Grand Strand doesn't have much in the way of Sea Islands, but there is Sandy Island between the Waccamaw and Pee Dee Rivers, which is a 9,164-acre island that had eight rice plantations on it, and some 120 slave descendants still live there. The Gullah Geechee culture has extended throughout the Grand Strand area as descendants moved around. A modern-day form of the pidgin is especially notable in both blacks and whites who grew up together in isolated areas.

As for Gullah food, it is still abundantly evident at local tables. As pointed out by Jesse Edward Gantt Jr. and Veronica Davis Gerald in *The Ultimate Gullah Cookbook*, its foundation came from weekly slave rations that were prepared using many African recipes and methods. When slaves gardened and hunted, it was natural to cook their harvests as their African and Caribbean ancestors taught them.

The slaves' sheer numbers—accounting for 90 percent of the South Carolina population in the mid-1700s—made it inevitable that their recipes would become traditional in southern cooking, especially since so many of them taste wonderful.

In many cases, African and Gullah food terms created English words that are still in use today. Word origin references tell us the slang term for peanut, "goober," comes from the Bantu and Kongo word *nguba*. The Umbundu word for okra is *ochinggombo*, which is where we get "gumbo," a soup with okra as a primary ingredient. Cooter originated from the Bambara and Malinke word for turtle, which is *kuta*.

Native Americans and white colonists ate sweet potatoes in South Carolina long before African slaves were brought here, but a popular (although technically incorrect) term for them—yams—has Portuguese, Spanish and African Fulani origins. Gullah slaves roasted them in hot ashes in hearths, boiled them in stews and eventually made biscuits out of them and turned them into sweet potato pies.

Rice, of course, was and is a staple of Gullah cuisine. Many slaves worked in African rice fields before they were brought to the United States, and they continued living and working in a rice culture. Pots of rice were cooked practically every day. Daily rice consumption continues today in many families, including the Gullah red rice, which is flavored with and colored by tomatoes.

African slaves cooked rice so that each grain is separate and firm yet tender, and that tradition continues in Georgetown and Horry Counties. Each cook prides him or herself on knowing how to cook a perfect pot of rice. Sandra Oliver noted that this way of cooking rice became known as "the Carolina method."

Collards, or collard greens, which are commonly attributed as having African roots, were probably already growing in South Carolina when slaves arrived. Ancient Greeks grew and ate them, and they were eaten throughout Europe in subsequent centuries. Known as a "cole" vegetable, both collards and cabbage are typical in Gullah cuisine. Part of the experience of enjoying collards the Gullah way is also drinking the juices—or likker—in which the greens are cooked.

"Every farm prides itself on the best collards," said Benjamin "B.B." Johnson of Georgetown. "You cut the middle portion [the ribs] out—that's hard to cook. You chop them up and cook them with whatever meat you desire, like a neckbone, ham or seasoned meats you buy at the store…when we cured the pork, then the seasoning that you put on the meat is already clinging to it for cooking. Sometimes we'd freeze [the collards] to help with the tenderness before you cook them."

Black-eyed peas are a variety of cowpea, or field pea, but neither one is actually a pea—they're both beans. They were "cultivated since pre-historic times in China and India," according to the Library of Congress, and they came to the United States with slave traders on the West Africa/West Indies/America route in the late seventeenth to early eighteenth century. Like peanuts, black-eyed peas were at first considered inferior food by whites, until they were hungry at the end of the Civil War and discovered that they were good eating.

Today, field peas and rice make up a traditional good luck dish called Hoppin' John, eaten by many southerners on New Year's Day. The peas' black spots are thought to represent coins that will invoke wealth for the New Year. They're often accompanied by collards on the New Year's dinner table, and their green color represents folding money.

Watermelons are indigenous to southern Africa, but when people from other lands discovered their cool, sweet juiciness, their cultivation spread around the world. Native Americans were growing watermelons before African slaves arrived, but since the slaves were familiar with them, they eagerly grew them as well. It didn't take long for everyone living in the colonial South to appreciate a cool slice of watermelon on a hot July afternoon.

Often slaves were given the less desired cuts of meat after their masters took the choice parts. The slaves were left with intestines, stomachs and other organs along with tails, hooves and heads. Some delicious dishes sprang from this ignoble start. Chitterlings, or chitlins, are pig intestines that are boiled or fried. Hog maw is a delicious dish of tripe, or pig stomach, cooked with potatoes and served over rice. They made headcheese and oxtail, and many of these dishes are still made in private homes and are available in some soul food and country cooking restaurants.

Charles and Aun Johnson, Georgetown County natives, serve many heritage foods they grew up eating at their restaurant on Front Street in

Georgetown called Aunny's Country Kitchen. Aun can track her family by name to her great-grandmother, Lorine Sherill, whose father was a full-blooded Native American, although she doesn't know to which tribe he belonged. Her great-great-grandmother, she said, was a slave. Charles said that his daughter has traced the family roots back to northern Europe and West Africa.

One of the dishes they serve at Aunny's is hog maw, made with pig stomach. "I learned to make hog maw from my mother [Sadie Johnson]," he said. "She taught me to cook from a young age…she taught me how to do chitlins and hog maw and collard greens…It was the throwaway from the hog, what the slave owners didn't want. That's how we got the pig feet, pig tail, hog's head cheese, chitlins. Hog's head cheese is a big delicacy in the black community."

Charles said that cooking hog maw to proper tenderness takes up to eleven hours of simmering on the stovetop. He starts off with "a lot of liquid" that boils down. "Chitlins don't take as much time to cook," he noted. "It's not as tough of a meat. Most African Americans combine the two—Chitlins and Hog Maw."

The couple enjoys making and eating catfish stew, crab cakes, shrimp in butter sauce and fried chicken. Aun remembers her great-grandmother cooking blackbirds, eel and raccoon, which she says is an oily meat that makes a tasty rice pilaf.

"What I remember the most eating while growing up is fried chicken and rice, with gravy," Aun said. "Mother would brown some onions in the pan with just a little oil and pour water in until it thickens, with flour. Sunday was always chicken, collard greens, rice and mac and cheese.

"And beans—we grew up on all those. I think lima beans was the number one beans in our heritage. Everyone made a pot of lima beans; it went a long way."

"I'm a fan of great northern beans," Charles said. "Every Monday I make a pot of great northern beans. I flavor them with ham, neckbone. The key ingredient is almost equal parts smoked neckbones and fresh neckbones. If you don't have equal, it's going to throw the taste off some."

"And you know what I like in the beans?" Aun asked. "Pig tail. Smoked pig tail and fresh. Just like Charles said, you have to do a combination of both. It just gives it a good flavor."

Charles said that he and his siblings couldn't afford to buy candy, so for sweets they would gather pecans, shell them and sauté them in butter and brown sugar. They also ate fresh figs "right off the trees" and turned them into preserves.

Aun's mother, Jane Goings, grew up on King Street in Georgetown. She remembered as a child eating catfish stew with onions and white gravy, stewed sturgeon, fried squid and okra soup.

"Macaroni and cheese—that was something you had every Sunday," Goings said. "Also fried chicken, definitely, and candy yams, okra soup, cabbage, biscuits and cornbread…My grandmother would make bread pudding with old dry white store-bought bread. She would soak it in milk, and she would put in it sugar, egg, raisins and a little cinnamon. She would bake it at 350 for forty minutes or so."

Goings makes the desserts at Aunny's Country Kitchen. She makes her grandmother's bread pudding with a few additions, such as diced apple, pineapple and fruit cocktail. She also makes sweet potato pie and old-fashioned pound cake the way her aunt taught her.

HOG MAW (PORK STOMACH)

Charles Johnson, Georgetown

5 pounds pork stomach
1 medium onion, chopped
1 medium bell pepper, chopped
3 stalks celery, chopped
3 white potatoes, peeled and diced
¼ cup vinegar
½ cup hot sauce
salt, pepper and seasoning salt to taste
½ raw onion, diced

In a large pot, bring pork stomach to a boil for about 2½ hours. Add remaining ingredients except for the diced raw onion. Cook over medium heat for about another 2½ hours. The longer they cook, the more tender they become. When the maws are tender, add raw onion to give a little crunchiness. Serve over white rice or along with hot sauce.

Chapter 5

PILAU AND CHICKEN BOG

While African slaves brought their knowledge of rice agriculture to Grand Strand kitchens, it was their native cuisine in addition to the entrenched foodways of their French Huguenot slave masters that firmly planted pilau (pronounced *per*-low by locals) in Georgetown County kitchens.

Even Native Americans adopted and loved pilau. Chicora chief Clyde Strickland said that one of his nation's traditional rice and meat recipes came about after rice plantations moved into the area.

The word "pilau" derives from pilaf, a Persian word for a dish composed of meat and rice. Pilau was a familiar dish to the original 170 Huguenot families who escaped religious persecution in their homeland and immigrated to South Carolina in the late 1680s. While searching for new careers, they learned that rice grew well in the area. Knowing how valuable the crop was in Europe and understanding how such a grain could provide a nutritious boost for their own diets, they and other New World residents set about growing the grain.

Early rice planters did not have great success until they learned that West Africans were skilled at the tidal flow rice-growing method that could be replicated along Georgetown County's six freshwater coastal rivers. As related by James Fitch in *Pass the Pilau, Please*, many of those Africans brought to America had already labored in African rice fields, so they came well trained. It wasn't long before Georgetown County was producing half the annual national rice crop.

And they ate pilau—meat and rice—which was considered comfort food to masters and slaves. For slaves, who had few cooking utensils, it was a familiar and nutritious one-pot dish that they could put together from their food rations and supplement with foraging. Plantation owners tasted the flavors of their heritage and the success of their wealth. The dish's popularity extended well beyond the more than 150 Georgetown County rice plantations and soon was a favorite food among all classes of the area's residents.

Horry County Museum director Walter Hill grew up in the Georgetown County house where Elizabeth "Bessie" Allston Pringle lived and wrote after the Civil War. It was the summer home at Chicora Wood Plantation and is smaller than her father's grand mansion. Hill said, "All around the world, people have a one-pot dish using a local meat and a local grain. I think it's interesting to see how we used it here, with rice, and with the Huguenots coming in here."

Pilau (which is also spelled by locals "perlow," "purlow," "pirlau," "perlau," "perlo," "perloo" and more) was and is made with many types of meat: chicken, marsh hens (clapper rails), squirrel, venison, duck, pork, dove, opossum and raccoon. Especially in previous centuries, the cook used whatever meat was handy. An especially creative spelling of pilau was published in naturalist William Bartram's account of his travels through South Carolina and other southern states: "We visited this bird isle, and some of our people taking sticks or poles with them, soon beat down, loaded themselves with these squabs and returned to camp; they were almost a lump of fat, and made us a rich supper; some we roasted and made others into a pilloe with rice: most of them, except the bitterns and tantali, were so excessively fishy in taste and smell, I could not relish them."

Some folks call the dish pilaf instead of pilau, and today, the classic preparation in Georgetown and Horry Counties uses chicken and sausage. Also, in Horry County it's called chicken bog, not pilau, and they have differences. "A chicken bog can be a pilau, but a pilau can never be a chicken bog," Hill said. The main differences between the two are rice texture and conformity of preparation methods. Pilau has a precise traditional recipe that results in separate and firm rice grains, and purists insist that any deviation isn't pilau. The rice in chicken bog usually is, well, boggier. The rice comes out stickier, which can be due to longer cooking times than pilau or the tendency to cook it in large quantities.

How chicken bog got its name and when the term came into use is a matter of speculation. The land in Horry and Georgetown Counties certainly is swampy and boggy, and the common practice of cooking it in large pots does result in meat bogged down in rice. It's reasonable to assume that sometime in

Pilau has been a Georgetown County specialty since the seventeenth century. *Photo by Matt Silfer, Silfer Studios.*

the 1800s, residents of Horry County familiar with pilau evolved the dish into their own interpretation with a name unique to their area.

What is certain is that chicken pilau is unique to Georgetown County and southern coastal areas down to Savannah, while chicken bog is unique to Horry County and extending a little into Pee Dee areas. "When you go anywhere else [in the South]," Hill said, "it's not recognized as pilau or bog. It's called chicken and rice."

Becky Ward Curtis of Georgetown remembered her father, Buster Camlin, making pilau with chicken—sometimes using just the backbone meat. "It always had fatback in it," she said. "And there were onions and pork sausage in the pilau."

In February 2013, Wayne Skipper, the farm manager at the Horry County Museum's L.W. Paul Living History Farm, and farm volunteer Levon Hucks cooked a pot of chicken bog for a blacksmiths' gathering. It was a chilly day, and a large cast-iron pot was set up over an outdoor fire. Hucks stirred the pot with a wood paddle, while Skipper added ingredients.

Skipper grew up on an Horry County farm and remembered his mother making the dish on cold winter days while the family sawed wood. "This time of year, we sawed wood for heating and to use on the farm," he said. "It was an all-day thing. We'd all go to the area my father chose, and my mother would take a cast-iron pot, chicken, rice, water, salt, black pepper and red pepper—all measured out. In the early days, they'd load that and go to the wood cutting place by mule and wagon and, later, on a tractor. She had a little rack she could set up the pot on and get the pot up on a brickbat. We'd stay out there all day and cut wood, and she'd have it ready for dinner."

His mother, Mary Dean Owens Skipper, didn't use sausage in her chicken bog because Skipper's father "enjoyed a very plain chicken taste. He actually didn't want anything in it but chicken, salt and pepper, side meat or fat back." The Skipper family farmed tobacco, and the end of the harvest was marked with a pot of chicken bog cooked by the barn.

Chicken bog is celebrated with a festival on the third Saturday in October in Loris, which is located in the western part of Horry County. A centerpiece of the festival is the Bog-Off, during which local cooks prepare chicken bog for sampling and to compete for cash, prizes and bragging rights.

Horry County historian and childhood Loris resident Catherine Lewis wrote that the Bog-Off is "the centerpiece of which is a contest for the best cook of the local food specialty. Chicken bog is a tasty blend of rice, chicken, sausage, and spices. Each cook uses some spice or other ingredient to make it a signature dish. The basic recipe for chicken bog is to boil a hen until the meat falls from the bone, remove the bones and cut up the meat, and cook rice in the broth (1 cup rice to 2 cups broth). Add to the rice and broth the meat of the chicken, sausage, and other seasonings."

Today, some people in Horry County use pork instead of chicken and call it hog bog. Walter Hill said that in Georgetown County, a pork and rice dish is called ham and rice, not pork pilau.

Owners of the Socastee Station restaurant in Myrtle Beach innovated with traditional chicken bog by forming it into balls and then battering and deep-frying them. Chicken Bog Balls are served with a creamy and spicy dipping sauce, and in 2013, they could be purchased at the restaurant, as well as at the Myrtle Beach Pelicans minor-league baseball field in downtown Myrtle Beach.

Walter Hill offered his family's traditional pilau recipe and said that the classic golden pilau color comes from onion caramelized in bacon fat.

TRADITIONAL GEORGETOWN COUNTY PILAU

Walter Hill

"This is how my grandfather, my uncle and my mother—how we cook pilau in Georgetown County. Nine times out of ten, you're going to have more broth than you need. My wife freezes the excess. Back in the early days, you would have used a green sausage, a hard sausage, more like salami."

1 whole small chicken, duck, squirrel, pork butt, ham hock or 4–6 doves
water
3 cloves garlic, minced
salt and ground black pepper, to taste
1 pound bacon or salt pork, chopped
2 onions, chopped
1 pound smoked sausage, sliced
2 cups rice

Place your meat, bone-in, in a large pot and add water to cover. Add garlic, salt and pepper. Bring to a boil, reduce heat to simmer and cook until meat is tender. Remove meat from pot and pull the meat from the bones. Remove the broth from the pot. Put your bacon or salt pork in the pot and cook until the fat starts to come out, then add your onions and sweat them. Add your sausage to start marrying the flavors. Put your other meat back in the pot and then add four cups of the broth. Stir the pot to get up any bits of meat or onion off the bottom and bring the broth to a boil. Add your rice, cover the pot and reduce the heat to a low simmer. After 20 minutes, turn off the heat. Don't take the lid off the pot until after 10 more minutes, when the rice should be perfectly done.

CHICKEN BOG FOR A CROWD

Wayne Skipper, Horry County

3 packages mini smoked sausage links
2 cups fatback, chopped
½ stick butter
½ cup pickled cayenne peppers, chopped
½ cup chow chow
1 pound smoked sausage, chopped
2 large onions, chopped
2 eggs
salt
1 stockpot full of boneless chicken thigh meat
20 cups water
10 cups rice

Set the pot over a small hardwood fire and add sausage, fatback and a little butter. Cook and stir until the grease is released. Add the peppers, chow chow, smoked sausage, onions and eggs. Stir so it doesn't scorch, until the onions are sweated. Add salt to taste, about ¼ cup. Add chicken and continue cooking and stirring until chicken is mostly cooked through. Add water and bring to a boil. Add rice and stir, and get it hot all around real fast until the rice boils. Stir it two more times and then take the pot off the fire and set it aside. Let it sit for one hour and don't open it, not even a crack. This method can only be done with a cast-iron pot with a tight-fitting lid.

Chicken Pilaf

Aun Johnson, Georgetown

1 whole chicken
water
½ cup cooking oil
2 cups mixed peppers, onions, celery, chopped
2 tablespoons Kitchen Bouquet
salt, pepper and seasoning salt, to taste
2½ pounds par-boiled rice
4 smoked sausages, chopped (optional)

In a large pot, boil chicken in water until done. When chicken is done, take as much of the bones and skin out as possible, then add oil, vegetables, Kitchen Bouquet and seasonings. Bring back to boil and add the rice, making sure the water covers the rice by about 2 inches. Bring back to a boil and continue boiling for about 3–4 minutes, or until you can see the rice. If using sausage, add it now. Cover pot with a piece of aluminum foil and a lid. Simmer over very low heat until rice is done.

Chapter 6

REVOLUTIONARY DINING

General Francis Marion (1732–1795), known as the "Swamp Fox," was a Revolutionary War hero who fought guerrilla warfare in the swampy Grand Strand area. He was also a farmer, and he knew the value of sweet potatoes, which grow well in the Grand Strand's sandy soil and are rich in protein and vitamins.

Actually, both the British and Patriot troops understood the nutritional and mobile value of sweet potatoes. Since area farms and plantations grew the tubers in abundance and stored them in outdoor potato banks, stealing them was an easy job for foraging soldiers. They called these missions "rooting parties," according to *The Life of Francis Marion* by W. Gilmore Simms:

> *His expeditions were frequently long, and his men, hurrying forth without due preparation, not unfrequently suffered much privation from want of food. To guard against this danger, it was their habit to watch his cook. If they saw him unusually busied in preparing supplies of the rude, portable food, which it was Marion's custom to carry on such occasions, they knew what was before them, and provided themselves accordingly. In no other way could they arrive at their general's intentions.*
>
> *His favorite time for moving was with the setting sun, and then it was known that the march would continue all night. Before striking any sudden blow, he has been known to march sixty or seventy miles, taking no other food in twenty-four hours, than a meal of cold potatoes and a draught of cold water. The latter might have been repeated. This was truly a Spartan*

process for acquiring vigor. Its results were a degree of patient hardihood, as well in officers as men, to which few soldiers in any periods have attained.

These marches were made in all seasons. His men were badly clothed in homespun, a light wear which afforded little warmth. They slept in the open air, and frequently without a blanket. Their ordinary food consisted of sweet potatoes, garnished, on fortunate occasions, with lean beef. Salt was only to be had when they succeeded in the capture of an enemy's commissariat; and even when this most necessary of all human condiments was obtained, the unselfish nature of Marion made him indifferent to its use. He distributed it on such occasions, in quantities not exceeding a bushel, to each Whig family; and by this patriarchal care, still farther endeared himself to the affection of his followers.

By 1780, Simms wrote, Marion's soldiers were a group of about 150 bedraggled Patriots with little ammunition who were living off the land. One night, with his camp pitched near the head of the Waccamaw River, a sixteen-year-old boy named Judge James had supper with the camp. James later wrote:

The dinner was set before the company by the General's servant, Oscar, partly on a pine log and partly on the ground. It consisted of lean beef, without salt, and sweet potatoes. The author had left a small pot of boiled hominy in his camp, and requested leave of his host to send for it, and the proposal was gladly acquiesced in. The hominy had salt in it, and proved, though eaten out of the pot, a most acceptable repast. The General said but little, and that was chiefly what a son would be most likely to be gratified by, in the praise of his father. We had nothing to drink but bad water; and all the company appeared to be rather grave.

But sweet potatoes helped keep them alive, healthy and victorious.

Other Revolutionary officers could write home for more luxurious provisions. Thomas Pinckney (1750–1828), the younger son of Charles Pinckney and Eliza Lucas Pinckney, was a captain of engineers during the American Revolution. Later, he was a major general during the War of 1812 and was governor of South Carolina for two years. His family of rice plantation owners were wealthy.

Pinckney wrote home to his sister, Harriott Pinckney Horry, on October 10, 1775, while he was stationed at Fort Johnson in Charles Town and asked for "some herbs to make Tea for the sick People, and about Sugar enough to replenish my little cannister." A postscript added, "A few Limes to make Punch with would not be disagreeable."

In November 1775, Thomas wrote to his sister that while traveling afield in South Carolina, he was turned away hungry by a homeowner who had "a fine fore Quarter of Venison Smoking at the Fire and some noble Potatoes in the ashes." His next stop, however, proved to have an accommodating host, who served him "such good Beef and Mutton, such nice Peach Pyes and cream and delicate Syllabubs."

Syllabubs are cold dairy desserts a little like modern-day floats made of blended cream and wine, and they sometimes included other ingredients like orange or lime juices, refined sugar or rosemary. They were put in special glasses that allowed the liquid part to be sipped through a spout, and the whipped cream topping was eaten with a spoon.

In February 1776, Thomas asked his sister for "A few Pounds of fresh Beef or any fresh meat" and "Wine by the Dozn." and thanked her for sending a turkey. In October 1776, he moved to Sullivan's Island and asked Harriott to send a few pounds of fresh or salted butter.

A long letter to his sister, written from Goochland County, Virginia, on January 31, 1777, makes note of "Captain Short, an honest hearty fat little Man of about 200 Weight, he eats with as much Perseverance and drinks Juleps with as much success as any Man I have ever met with." He also mentioned "a hearty Breakfast on big Hominy and a Variety of good things," as well as being soaked by a heavy rain, "the bad Effects of which we counteracted with a copious Dram of excellent Peach Brandy (which by the way is the most delicious Cordial that is made)."

On July 31, 1777, back at Fort Moultrie, Thomas thanked his sister for sending ham and melons, and on September 15, 1777, he said that they partook of "Turkey, Ham, Roast Mutton, Boil'd Mutton, Beef Stakes."

On May 23, 1778, Thomas wrote to Harriott from Fort Howe on the Altamaha River in Georgia and described camp life, which included bacon pilau:

> Our style of living here is pretty Uniform we rise early, breakfast on boiled rise, beef Steaks, & water, by way of Coffee, lounge about the Camp when off Duty 'till one or two oClock, commonly get at Catfish, sometimes a Trout or Bream with a repetition of our Breakfast for Dinner; repeat the lounge 'till supper when we fare as sumptuously as we did at dinner. I forgot to mention that we have some Bacon Which now and then affords a Pilaw without a fowl, & by the Bounty Of General Howe have still some Rum left.

From Purysburg, South Carolina, Thomas wrote on April 19, 1779, that he and three hundred other soldiers "have plenty of green Pease, Sallad, & other Vegetables, Meat, Milk, bread, Rice in short every thing but Rum, which is rather scarce."

In 1780, Thomas was wounded near Camden and captured by the British. He was a prisoner for more than a year, and on September 7, 1780, he wrote home to his mother, Eliza Lucas Pinckney, and urged her to send no more parcels with limes in them because they were too perishable. On the same day, he wrote to Harriott and asked her to send two or three dozen bottles of "good Port Wine" and to "have it sent only as far as Mount Joseph I can have it forwarded thence by two or three Bottles at a Time."

Eliza and her daughter, Harriott, also sent supplies to Eliza's older son, Charles Cotesworth Pinckney (1746–1825), who was commander of the First Regiment of the South Carolina troops in 1776 and was an aide-de-camp to George Washington in 1777–78. He returned to South Carolina as a commander, was captured by the British in Charles Town in 1780 and was a prisoner until 1782. They sent Charles rum, port wine, sugar, tea, rice, corn and many medicinal home remedies such as willow bark and rhubarb.

Harriott's husband, Daniel Huger Horry Jr., was a wealthy plantation owner who served under General Francis Marion during the Revolutionary War. He helped supply the Patriots with provisions. At the end of the war in 1783, he sent a bill to the U.S. government for a long list of supplies, including thousands of pounds of beef and pork, thousands of bushels of rice, a few sheep and corn.

Chapter 7
GEORGE WASHINGTON ATE HERE

The United States of America was new, and its first president, George Washington, made a southern tour during his first of two terms in office. He arrived in South Carolina on Wednesday, April 27, 1791, three days after Easter.

Washington's account in his personal diary notes where he ate and who fed him, but he didn't go into detail about what was served. Re-creating typical fare of the times and places, here's a logical researched estimation of his menus.

Washington traveled in "a light coach drawn by four horses," wrote Catherine Lewis in an article about Little River. "The little cavalcade consisted of his saddle horse and one extra, four more coach horses, and a baggage wagon with two horses. Besides the president there were his aide, Major William Jackson, a valet de chambre [manservant] and four men to drive and look after the horses. There were no advance men, no reservations. Washington accepted whatever accommodations the roadside provided."

In those days, a public place to eat and drink in South Carolina was called a "Carolina ordinary," and they were identified by having "a jug suspended from a pole" out front, as Sandra Oliver noted, quoting from eighteenth-century traveler John Bernard.

Imagine the surprise of innkeepers and ordinary owners when President Washington came through the door! However, there is evidence that some people—such as private homeowners—knew he was coming. Harriott

Pinckney Horry of Hampton Plantation, which was the president's last stop in the Grand Strand area before continuing to Charleston, definitely knew of the upcoming visit.

In a letter to George Washington dated April 14, 1791, Horry wrote, "Sir, I heard with great pleasure that your Excellency purposed favoring this part of the Continent with a visit, and as my house on Santee is in your rout to Charleston If you will do me the honor of making it a stage I shall be extremely happy to show your Excellency the respect with which I am, Your Excellency's, Most Obedient Servant, Harriott Horry."

George Washington and his party crossed over the North Carolina line into South Carolina at 12:30 p.m. on April 27. They dined at

President George Washington (1732–1799) visited Horry and Georgetown Counties in 1791, during his first term in office. This circa 1899 engraving by S. Arlent Edwards (1861–1938) was made from a 1790 painting by John Trumbull (1756–1843). *Picture Collection, the New York Public Library, Astor, Lenox and Tilden Foundations.*

a private home owned by Revolutionary War veteran James G. Cochran and then spent the night at an inn owned by Jeremiah Vereen just south of present-day North Myrtle Beach.

The president wrote in his journal, "To this house we were directed as a Tavern, but the proprietor of it either did not keep one, or would not acknowledge it—we therefore were entertained (& very kindly) without being able to make compensation." The building was formerly a public house, but it was a private residence at the time President Washington visited, and Vereen would not allow the president to pay for anything.

As detailed in Frank E. Grizzard's *George Washington: A Biographical Companion*, the president was fond of rum punch, beer, hard cider, porter and wines, especially Madeira. Likely, Jeremiah Vereen had at least a few of those beverages on hand to refresh the president after a long day's travel. Sam Vereen, a direct descendant of Jeremiah Vereen, said that family lore has it that the president so enjoyed the rum he was served that night that he sent an aide back a few days later to fetch more.

As for the food served, the meal likely included cured ham, sausages and, since they were so close to the coast, fresh seafood. "I'm quite certain there was some duck and some venison involved, because [our family] did like duck," Russell Vereen said. Russell is Sam Vereen's son, and since 1993, he has owned and operated Russell's Seafood Grill and Raw Bar in Murrells Inlet. "Our family has always hunted and fished and [butchered] hogs." However, it wasn't quite deer season, so salt pork, sausage and fish are more logical assumptions. Russell Vereen said that fresh fish served in April 1791 would have been netted, and likely springtime catches would have been flounder, spot or mullet.

On Thursday the twenty-eighth, Vereen piloted the group across Singleton Swash. This is where, more than one hundred years later, after a hurricane, a man found a brass plate a little bigger than a dollar bill inscribed with "Geo. Washington." The plate was later stolen from a Myrtle Beach office safe, according to Horry County Museum director Walter Hill.

The group traveled twenty-one miles along the coast down along Ye Olde Kings Highway. The travelers had dinner at a private home owned by "Mr. Pauley," who was George Pawley of Pawleys Island, for whom the island is named. Known as America's oldest seaside resort area, Pawleys Island is a secluded and lovely beach area where wealthy planters purchased land from George Pawley to build summer retreats. The planters and their families routinely left the plantations the last week of May and didn't return until the first week of November to escape summer heat, the stink of stagnant flooded rice fields and the still waters that resulted in malaria-infested mosquitoes.

In 1791, a springtime Pawleys Island lunch most likely included fresh seafood. Since they were in rice country, the fish was surely served accompanied by or over rice.

In a letter dated April 28, 1791, John Rutledge sent word to Thomas Pinckney at Hampton Plantation: "Dr Sir, The President arrived here this morning he will go Tomorrow to George town & intends dining at Mrs Horrys on Sunday Genl Moultrie requests that you will have your Boats at Santee to assist in carrying over the Presidents Horses. I am Sir, Yours &, J Rutledge Junr."

That night, George Washington and his companions stayed with Dr. Henry Collins Flagg, chief of the medical staff under General Nathanael Greene during the Revolutionary War, at his home at Brookgreen Plantation.

On Friday the twenty-ninth, "We left Doctr. Flagg's about 6 o'clock, and arrived at Captn. Wm. Alston's on the Waggamau [Waccamaw] to Breakfast." Revolutionary War veteran Captain William Alston owned Clifton Plantation located just north of Georgetown.

It was well known that George Washington loved hoecakes with honey and butter for breakfast, as documented by Martha Washington's granddaughter, Nelly Custis Lewis. Her recipe for hoecakes was on display at Mount Vernon from February 2012 through August 2013, and it involves cornmeal, yeast, water and egg to make a sort of cornmeal pancake. Considering that southerners are known for cornbread and many variations, it's highly likely that the Alstons' cook whipped up some hoecakes for the president and served them with honey or corn syrup.

An interesting kitchen utensil survives from Clifton Plantation: a wafer iron, which was donated to Brookgreen Gardens in Murrells Inlet by Mrs. Frederick Wentworth Ford. Robin Salmon, Brookgreen's vice-president of art and historical collections and curator of sculpture, said that wafer irons were used for hundreds of years and can be traced back to European, Scandinavian, Middle Eastern and Asian kitchens. In the United States, they were used from the mid-eighteenth century through the beginning of the twentieth century.

Salmon added that some wafers were made for use during church communion, but others were a type of light bread eaten in Europe at the ends of meals to aid digestion. The irons are embossed with decorations and patterns that could have had religious or familial significance, such as a coat of arms, or simply had pretty floral or geometric designs. "[O]nly the most wealthy could afford to have them," Salmon said. "Eventually, it became more of a dessert (like a thin cookie). Larger wafers were also rolled or curled and flavored fillings were added."

Made of cast iron, the tong device has circles on its ends. After being preheated, batter was placed on one of the circles and the tongs were pressed closed before being put in or over hot coals. It was flipped once before the wafer was done. Excess batter that had squeezed out was trimmed off, the iron was opened and the wafer was loosened with a knife before being peeled off with the fingers and set on a board to cool. As hearth cooking gave way to stoves, Salmon said, wafer irons (and rectangular-ended cast-iron waffle irons, which had the same design) were set on top of hot stoves to cook.

The diary continues:

Captn. Alston is a Gentleman of large fortune and esteemed one of the neatest Rice planters in the State of S. Carolina and a proprietor of the most valuable

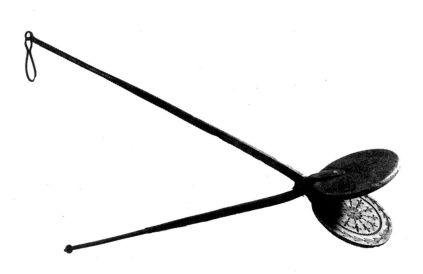

Wealthy families used wafer irons such as this one from Clifton Plantation to create embossed bread-like treats. Gift of Mrs. Frederick Wentworth Ford to the Brookgreen Gardens Collection. *Brookgreen Gardens, Murrells Inlet, South Carolina.*

ground for the culture of this article.—His house which is large, new, and elegantly furnished stands on a sand hill, high for the Country, with his Rice fields below; the contrast of which with the lands back of it, and the Sand & piney barrens through which we had passed is scarecely to be conceived.

At Captn. Alston's we were met by General Moutree, Col. Washington & Mr. Rutledge (son of the present Chief Justice of S. Carolina) who had come out that far to escort me to town.—We dined and lodged at this Gentlemans and Boats being provided we the next morning (Saturday, 30th), Crossed the Waggamau to Georgetown by descending the River three miles—at this place we were reed. Under a Salute of Cannon, & by a Company of Infantry handsomely uniformed.—I dined with the Citizens in public; and in the afternoon was introduced to upwards of 50 ladies who had assembled (at a Tea party) on the occasion.

It is commonly believed, but not proven, that the tea party took place at the Stewart-Parker House, which is where Georgetown residents say it's most likely the president stayed while in town, according to the property's director, Cindy Kinder. Built by Robert Stewart in about 1740, it was sold to Daniel Tucker in 1787, who was the president's host.

The circa 1740 Stewart-Parker House is the riverfront home where, according to local legend, President George Washington stayed when he visited Georgetown in 1791. The house is owned by the Colonial Dames of South Carolina and is available for tours and special events. *Georgetown Postcard Collection, Georgetown County Library, Georgetown, South Carolina.*

So what would be served at a tea party honoring of the president of the United States? Tea of course, but it would not have been grown locally. According to the South Carolina Information Highway, tea was not grown in South Carolina until 1799, at Middleton Place (at that time called Middleton Barony) near Charleston.

Since Georgetown was a bustling little town with several shops, it would have been easy to find elegant foods to serve for tea. A banquet served in Georgetown in early May 1905 was reported in the *Georgetown Times*, and the meal was "in keeping with the old time honored traditions" of Georgetown's Winyah Indigo Society, which was established in 1753. Grover Cleveland attended that anniversary event, and although he was no longer president then, it was surely a presidential occasion.

Since the 1905 banquet was an anniversary gala celebrating its long history, and the newspaper article reported that the meal features historic foods, it is logical that the same sorts of foods would have been fed to President George Washington when he was in town. The president visited Georgetown at the end of April, and the Winyah Indigo Society banquet was at the beginning of May, so even the same garden produce of garden peas and new potatoes would have been available.

The 1905 menu lists Blue Point oysters on the half shell, boiled bass with sauce blanche, terrapin soup, sherry, celery, olives, pickles, salted almonds, roast turkey, cranberry sauce, beef à la mode, new potatoes, rice, green peas, macaroni and asparagus. Beef à la mode was a bacon-wrapped pot roast marinated in wine and brandy for several hours before being braised. Other popular party foods of the day included shrimp pie, chicken salad and Charlotte Russe, which is custard surrounded by ladyfingers.

Today, the Stewart-Parker House is open to the public; it's next door to the Kaminski House Museum. The Stewart-Parker House is owned and operated by the Colonial Dames of South Carolina.

The president made a few remarks about Georgetown and its residents in his journal:

> *George Town seems to be in the shade of Charleston—It suffered during the War by the British, having had many of its Houses burnt. It is situated on a pininsula betwn. the River Waccamaw & Sampton Creek about 15 miles from the Sea—a bar is to be passed, over which not more than 12 feet water can be brot. Except at Spring tides; which (tho' the Inhabitants are willing to entertain different ideas,) must ever be a considerable let to its importance; especially if the cut between the Santee & Cooper Rivers, should ever be accomplished.*
>
> *The Inhabitants of this place (either unwilling or unable) could give no account of the number of Souls in it, but I should not compute them at more than 5 or 600.—Its chief export, Rice.*

On Sunday, May 1, 1791, George Washington left Georgetown about 6:00 a.m. and headed for Charleston (Charles Town became Charleston in 1783), stopping for breakfast at Hampton Plantation with Harriott Pinckney Horry, the widow of Revolutionary War veteran Colonel Daniel Horry. As noted earlier, she was a wealthy rice plantation owner, and she was expecting the visit.

This is where the account of what the president ate while in South Carolina strikes documentary gold. As mentioned in a previous chapter, Harriott Horry wrote a cookbook published as *A Colonial Plantation Cookbook: The Receipt Book of Harriot Pinckney Horry, 1770*. While there is no solid documentation of what Mrs. Horry fed the president, her cookbook gives us solid assumptions.

In the cookbook's introduction, written by Richard J. Hooker, he notes:

The foods available within South Carolina were uneven in quantity and quality. Milk and cheese were generally lacking except to the well-to-do. The pork and barnyard fowls, fed on corn and rice, were rated good, but the beef, veal, and mutton were "middling" or inferior because, said one man, the cattle and sheep were not fattened but rather slaughtered direct from the thin pastures. From nearby fields and waters, however, there was a plentiful supply of venison, wild turkeys, geese, ducks, and other wild fowl. Terrapin were found in all the ponds, and at times ships arrived from the West Indies with huge sea turtles. Fish were often scarce and expensive, but oysters, crabs and shrimp could be bought cheaply.

Vegetables were available in season and were preserved for the winter months. Travelers noticed that the "long" (sweet) potatoes were a great favorite and there were also white potatoes, pumpkins, various peas and beans, squashes, cucumbers, radishes, turnips, carrots, and parsnips among other vegetables.

Rice, of course, was predominant on the menu and in recipes, along with corn in its many variations. "Lowcountry dwellers grew and enjoyed a profusion of fruits," Hooker wrote, including "oranges, peaches, citrons, pomegranates, lemons, pears, apples, figs, melons, nectarines and apricots as well as a variety of berries" such as strawberries and raspberries.

Nutmeg, mace, pepper and cloves were Harriot Pinckney's favorite spices, and mace is noted in many recipes of the time. Today, mace is still a principal ingredient in traditional preparations of she-crab soup. "Quite a few of Harriott's recipes call for a lavish use of butter, milk and cream," Hooker noted. "This was also in line with English practices, though only a few South Carolinians would have had the ingredients to work with. But Hampton in 1772 had forty cows."

The 1790 census lists Hampton Plantation as having 340 slaves, so Harriott had plenty of kitchen help to prepare an elaborate presidential breakfast. So what would Harriott have served the president of the United States? Typical colonial breakfasts were simple meals with cornbread and cornmeal mush, with molasses, milk, tea, hard cider or beer, but it is unlikely that Harriott stopped there for such an esteemed guest. She would have served the best of her best, of course, which would definitely have included Hampton Plantation's best rice.

Harriott probably had cornbread, or the president's beloved hoecakes, on the table since she was acquainted with him and likely knew his dining preferences. Several varieties of yeast rolls were in her repertoire, along with rice bread, and she would have set out her finest jams and marmalades to accompany the baked goods.

Her freshest sausages, bacon and ham would have been available, and since she had advance notice of the president's arrival, Harriott could have ordered that a hog or calf be butchered. In her travels, Harriott made note of remarking on different area's fresh fish, and she may have wanted the president to sample her area's freshwater fishes and seafood. Grits or hasty pudding, with plenty of butter and cream, was in her repertoire, so perhaps George Washington got to taste fish and grits.

Bops

From A Colonial Plantation Cookbook: The Receipt Book of Harriott Pinckney Horry, 1770

> *Take about a pound of Flour and rub into it a pap spoonful of Butter then add as much Milk as will make it into a very thick Batter then put it into a marble Mortar and beat it till 'tis quite light drop it upon tin Sheets (about a large spoonful in a drop) and bake them. They are to be split and butter'd.*
> *N.B. the Butter should be rub'd in the flour till you can't feel the Butter.*
> [A notation reads, "This is a misspelling for baps which was, and is, a small breakfast roll of Scotland."]

Sausages

From A Colonial Plantation Cookbook: The Receipt Book of Harriott Pinckney Horry, 1770

> *To 15 lb. Meat (9 lb. lean to 6 lb. fat.) pickd and chopd fine put ½ pint Salt one Table Spoonful Salt Peter finely pounded—2 Table Spoonsfull dried sage and 2 spoonful dried Thyme finely pounded, 1 handful green parsley chop'd fine ½ pepper ¼ All spice 1 Nutmeg and a pinch of Mace pounded all fine Season the Meat and let it lay all night and stuff them in the Morning. NB the Skin should be scraped very thin and every little film taken off.* [A notation says that this recipe is from Mrs. Motte.]

Chapter 8

1800–1861

B etween vastly wealthy plantation owners and their slaves was a middle class described by Elizabeth Allston Pringle in *Chronicles of Chicora Wood*:

> *These people, the yeomanry of the country, were the descendants of the early settlers, and those who fought through the Revolution. They were, as a general rule, honest, law-abiding, with good moral standards. Most of them owned land, some only a few acres, others large tracts, where their cattle and hogs roamed unfed but fat. Some owned large herds, and even the poorest usually had a cow and pair of oxen, while all had chickens and hogs—but never a cent of money. They planted corn enough to feed themselves and their stock, sweet potatoes, and a few of the common vegetables.*

Sweet potatoes continued to be a staple of South Carolina cuisine that reached across all classes. On September 8, 1806, Daniel Horry (who changed his name to Charles Lucas Pinckney) and his wife, Eleanore de la Tour-Maubourg Horry, sent a letter from Paris to Daniel's mother, Harriott Pinckney Horry, requesting that she ship them sweet potatoes from Hampton Plantation because "the empress," Josephine Bonaparte, was eager to have them:

> *If you can send us sweet potatoes, dear mother, either upon M Grant's return of some other opportunity, it would give us great pleasure; the empress has asked Charles for them insistently, and the ones that he*

brought with him arrived almost entirely rotten since the captain had undoubtedly put the chest that contained them at the bottom of the hold where the sea water spoiled them. To avoid this they should be packed in fine and very dry sand, and the chest should be wrapped in an oiled or waxed canvas.

In October 1807, he wrote back to say that the sweet potatoes arrived safety and that the empress approved of them.

While there were skirmishes with British ships along the southern coast during the War of 1812, the war mainly affected South Carolinians in that trade with Great Britain and France was restricted, including an embargo on the exportation of rice. Harriott Horry was unlucky enough to have a schooner loaded with corn near Port Royal in the summer of 1813, and two British ships burned the schooner and "carried off the Negroes belonging to it."

During the summer of 1812, Revolutionary War hero Peter Horry was the owner of four plantations in the Georgetown area. He wrote much during his lifetime, and that summer he wrote extensively in a journal while at his beach home on North Island in Winyah Bay. Those journal entries were detailed by Coastal Carolina University history professor Roy Talbert Jr. in his 1998 lecture on Horry.

As was customary at the time, Horry took with him by boat several slaves, a carriage and furniture. He also took livestock, including "his mules, a cow and calf, several hogs, ducks and chickens." Chiefly, amusement meant visiting with other island inhabitants and their guests, so food played a central role in the summer's entertainment.

"The white gentry on the island enjoyed a varied diet, although Horry complained, 'I can Get no Dainties here,'" Talbert wrote in a section of his lecture titled "Horry's Menu."

As families received shipments of fruits and vegetables from Georgetown, they shared with their friends. At one point, Horry worried that he had only "Water Mellions" to give away. He was the recipient of grapes, figs, pears, apples, and even oranges and limes from the West Indies. Other staples included rice, okra, snap beans, and Seewee beans, their word for our limas. The real delicacies came from the sea. Horry relished shrimp, oysters, clams, and crabs, and, to our environmental dismay, his very favorite dish was the egg of the sea turtle.

Horry's slaves fished for their own suppers, using pole nets and hooks and lines, and Talbert said that he wrote that catches included shrimp, mullet, crabs, whiting, croakers and catfish.

Ducks continued to be plentiful. In December 1822, Thomas Pinckney wrote to his sister, Harriott Horry, from the family's land on the Santee River that "we fare sumptuously every day on canvass back ducks." Pinckney said that this is the only meat he had in plenty following an 1822 hurricane.

In 1822, Myrtle Beach did not yet exist—the area was called Long Bay. Later it was called Wither—named for a family who owned much property in the area—before it was called New Town in the late 1800s. It didn't become Myrtle Beach until 1900, named for its many wax myrtle trees.

Present-day Conway, the Horry County seat, also changed names during this period. Originally named Kingston Township when it was laid out in 1732, it became Conwayborough (named for Revolutionary War hero Brigadier General Robert Conway) in 1801. In 1883, the name was shortened to Conway.

South of Myrtle Beach, John Tillman owned a few dozen slaves who worked on the Ark Plantation, which encompassed 3,200 acres. Now part of Horry County, in the early 1800s, the site was in the Georgetown District. While part of the plantation—about 190 acres—was devoted to rice growing, most of its fields were devoted to sweet potatoes. The spot is a good indicator of where Grand Strand soil changes from the swampy river tidal flows necessary for rice production to the sandy soil perfect for growing sweet potatoes. Tillman died in 1865, and the plantation was developed into an area known as Roach's Beach. Eventually, the name changed to Floral Beach before it became its present-day Surfside Beach in 1952.

Experimentation in different methods of food preservation began to emerge, such as using pyrolygneous acid, also called wood vinegar, which is a byproduct of charcoal production. Thomas Pinckney commented to his sister in an 1824 letter, "The Pyrolygneous acid will not preserve fish with the mercury at 90°."

It was also during this period that South Carolinians such as Harriott Pinckney Horry began to wonder if sugar cane could be grown at Hampton Plantation as it was in the West Indies. Her brother, Charles Cotesworth Pinckney, told her in an 1814 letter that he had heard of sugar cane being grown in Florida.

In the 1900 work *Cultivation of Sugar Cane*, author William C. Stubbs wrote, "The first sugar cane planted in South Carolina, according to the 'Southern Agriculturalist,' in its May number, 1828, was an experiment patch planted in 'Tivoli Garden,' in or near Charleston, by Philip Chartrand, in 1827." The crop caught on quickly. By 1829, an experimental one-acre plot "yielded 23,150 average sized stalks of cane," and in 1850, the U.S. Census reports showed that South Carolina produced 805,200 pounds of sugar. Production hit a peak in the nineteenth century on the 1870 census with 1,266,000 pounds of sugar and 436,882 gallons of molasses or syrup.

It was around this time that more people switched from hearth cooking to wood-burning stoves that also doubled as heaters, but they didn't really catch on for most South Carolinians until more efficient coal-burning models became popular after the Civil War.

Since colonists first settled South Carolina, bread was mixed up in long and narrow wood dough bowls, or bread bowls. The Chestnut family donated a large bread bowl (circa 1820) to the Horry County Museum. They were used regularly in area kitchens well into the twentieth century.

"That's what they were making biscuits in around here," said museum director Walter Hill.

You'd put your flour in there and your lard in there, and it was a matter of ease and convenience in making them without following a real defined recipe. You'd have your flour and lard and work those in, and then add water or milk, like mixing mortar for bricks. They had a surplus of flour at one end of the bowl, and if the dough was too wet, they'd slowly draw in flour to be the right consistency to roll out the biscuits. They'd roll them by hand and make them small or big, depending what your taste was. Then they'd take all the little "crusties" left over and dump them for the hogs. You ate biscuits for breakfast and dinner—biscuits and cornbread. When you got home from school, your snack was a biscuit.

South Carolina barbecue soon became more entrenched in local culinary traditions. Special occasions called for cooking a whole pig, and in the dog days of summer, watermelons were also usually part of the menu. Over time, the southern use of the word "barbecue" changed from the name of the meat-eating event to refer to the actual meat. The event became known as a pig pickin' because the meat is literally picked off the bones.

More and more paddle-wheel boats cruised up and down the area's rivers serving as transportation for goods and people. Many of them had wheels on their sides instead of on the rear so they could turn around at narrow river docks such as at Conway, and they were called side-wheelers. Paddle-wheelers and oceangoing steamships brought a wide variety of

Left: This mid-nineteenth-century cast-iron pot was donated to Brookgreen Gardens by E. Milby Burton. *Brookgreen Gardens, Murrells Inlet, South Carolina.*

Below: Bread bowls were convenient for pulling the desired amount of flour into the dough, and they were easier to clean than tables. Donated to the Horry County Museum by the Chestnut family. *Photo by Matt Silfer, Silfer Studios.*

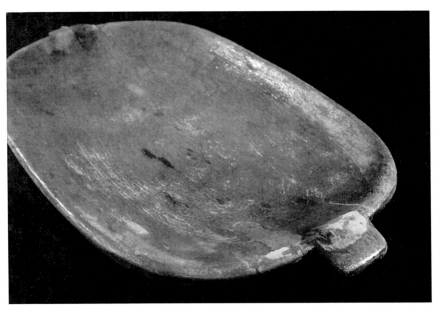

foods to Georgetown, where rice plantation owners were reaching the peaks of their wealth.

In September 1837, the *Georgetown Union* newspaper advertised a butcher who intended to provide his services to "the citizens of Georgetown and North Island" three times per week. "Canal Flour" and crackers were for sale, along with sugars from St. Croix, Muscovada and New Orleans, Jaya Coffee, London Mustard, Hyson Tea, smoked herrings, butter crackers, chocolate, almonds, raisins, wines, nutmegs, capers, mace, lime juice, lemon syrup and ginger. They even had bottled water, as "Saratoga Water" was sold in quarts and pints; "Champaigne" was also sold "in qts and pints."

In a January 1840 edition of the *Georgetown American* newspaper, E. Waterman listed for sale Irish potatoes and "Porto Rico" sugar, while J.G. Henning & Company had Prime Green Coffee. A lengthy agricultural article warns of the consequences of overdoing or underdoing the dunging of farmland.

Bessie Pringle aptly described the food of August 1840 at the Chicora Wood Plantation summer bungalow called the Meadows. She said that it was a particularly hot summer, and ice was a luxury that only people in "the North" had:

> *The Meadows was twenty miles from the nearest town and post-office, Georgetown, and everything had to be brought up by the plantation wagons and team. But milk and butter and cream were abundant, also poultry and eggs; and the Pedee furnished most delicious fish—bream and Virginia perch and trout. There were figs in abundance and also good peaches, but the latter were small and a good deal troubled with cuculio* [curculio, a type of weevil]. *They were, however, very good stewed, and my mother made quantities of delicious preserves from them.*
>
> *Around the house at Chicora grew luxuriant orangetrees, only the bittersweet; but these oranges make the nicest marmalade, so mama put up quantities of that for winter use. Her vegetable-garden was always full of delicious things—cucumbers, tomatoes, eggplant, and okra; and, as my father killed beef and mutton every week for use on the plantation, she had the very best soups and steaks; and there were always wild ducks to be had. Also, after August 1, there was venison in the house, for my father was devoted to deer-hunting. At the time the negroes understood preserving the venison in the hottest weather by exposing it to the broiling sun. I do not know what else they did, for it is now a lost art; but it was called "jerked venison" and was a delicious breakfast dish, when shaved very thin and*

broiled. They also preserved fish in the same way—called "corned fish"—
it was a great breakfast dish broiled. Besides all this, about the end of
August the rice-birds began to swarm over the rice, sucking out all the grain
when in the milk stage. This necessitated the putting out of bird-minders in
great numbers, who shot the little birds as they rose in clouds from the rice
at the least noise. These rice-birds are the most delicious morsels; smaller
than any other bird that is used for food, I think, so that a man with a good
appetite can eat a dozen, and I, myself, have eaten six…All these things
made living easy and abundant, for they came in great quantities.

A June 1847 advertisement in the *Winyah Observer* offers for sale "New
May Butter, Crackers and Cheese, Fresh Lard, Pickled Tongues, Smoked
Beef, Belogua Sausages, Pickles, Lemons, Oranges, Apples, Coconuts, Figs
and Raisins," plus "a lot of good N.C. Bacon."

June was when Grand Strand plantation families enjoyed time at the
beach, but the plantations were near enough for the men to go check on
the fields and other farm operations. A typical June 1847 day for Robert
F.W. Allston would be to leave Pawleys Island after an early breakfast and
be rowed over to Chicora Plantation. A house slave fed him a light lunch of
buttermilk and fruit, and he arrived back at Pawleys Island in time for "a
three-o'clock dinner."

Also before the Civil War, wealthy male plantation owners had a social
club called the Hot and Hot Fish Club in the Murrells Inlet area. It was
named for the practice of enjoying several courses of hot fresh fish.

By September 1854, advertisements in the *Pee Dee Times*, which covered
Georgetown County as well as the Pee Dee area of South Carolina, were
listing for sale

Heckers Farina; Orvi's Corn Starch; Gelatine; "Maccaroni"; Fresh Flour
from new Wheat; Self Raising Flour; Mocha, Java and Rio Coffee;
Smoked Beef and Tongues; Clarified, Crushed, Loaf and Brown Sugar;
Imperial, Hyson and Black Tea; Olive Oil; Cordials and Sauces; Superior
English Mustard; Fresh Lobsters in Cans; Ruta Baga and Dutch Turnip
Seeds; Flavoring Extracts, For Jellies, Creams, Pastry in rose, lemon,
vanilla and almond flavors; Fresh Tamarinds Put up in Honey; Butter
Cheese and Lard; Peas and Beans; Molasses from Havana; "New Orleans
Mollasses"; Corn & Bacon; Goshen Butter; Fulton Market Beef; Soda
Water; and Fine Liquors including Jean Louis, Sazarac, Pelvisin and
Peach Brandy, Madeira, Sherry and Port Wine, Heidseck, D'Aumate and

Grape "Champaign," Suppernong Wine, Jamaica and Grenada Rum, Scotch Whiskey and Old Monongahela Whiskey.

A few years before the Civil War began, the December 30, 1857 edition of the *Pee Dee Times* offered "Genuine Olive Oil" from Barcelona, mackerel, salmon, "Extra Sugar cured Hams," citron, prunes, figs, premium "Champaigne," pale Sherry wine, white wine vinegar, "Manhaden" fish, Worcestershire sauce, John Bull sauce, sardines and lobsters.

Chapter 9
THE WAR BETWEEN THE STATES

The American Civil War from 1861 to 1865 caused food deprivation for virtually all South Carolina residents and changed some eating habits.

The Grand Strand area's proximity to the ocean made it a prime area for salt production, which was increased during the Civil War to keep up with demand for supplying troops with food. In *Horry County, South Carolina, 1730–1993*, Catherine Lewis quoted the late local historian C.B. Berry on the matter:

> *The salt was manufactured by evaporating sea water and was a much needed commodity in the South at that time. To give you some idea of the size of the operation, the Yankee officer who commanded the forces that destroyed the factory, said there were about three thousand bushels of salt on hand and not knowing how to destroy it, had it mixed with sand so it could not be used. A salt water storage tank had a capacity of 100,000 gallons.*

The five-year war turned lives upside down and shook provisions out of South Carolinians' pantries, gardens and barnyards. The poorest farmers to the wealthiest plantation owners had their food stores plundered by troops from the Confederacy and the Union. These foraging soldiers were called "bummers."

Even Bessie Pringle, whose father, Robert F.W. Allston, was elected governor of South Carolina in 1856, was not immune to deprivation in her young, sheltered world. As detailed in local historian Charles Joyner's

Bummers were soldiers who foraged for food at the expense of South Carolina residents. Titled *The Bummer*, this illustration appeared in an 1865 issue of *Harper's Magazine*. *Picture Collection, the New York Public Library, Astor, Lenox and Tilden Foundations.*

introduction of her book, *A Woman Rice Planter*, he explained the plantation family's deprivations. Pringle was in her late teens and early twenties during the war and spent much of it in Charleston. In her diary, she wrote that the food at her school "has been poor," explaining, "We always have meat once a day; our supper consists of a huge tray of corn dodgers which is brought into the school-room and placed on the table, that we may help ourselves and the tray goes back empty."

As the war wore on, the Allstons moved eighty miles inland to a farm called Crowley Hill in Darlington County, where, Joyner noted, "They planted a garden to keep food on the tables, but other supplies became increasingly scarce."

In *Chronicles of Chicora Wood*, Bessie Pringle wrote of friends and neighbors giving them "supplies of every kind, milk, cream, vegetables, fruit, flowers, everything we did not have." Her brother, Charley, had been boarding at a country school, where he "lived for months on nothing but squash and hominy."

She also described the winter of 1863–64 at the end of her father's life (he died in April 1864), when they sat together at night and *had milk and potatoes, with sassafras tea for supper, and it was very good. One who has never had to depend on sassafras tea does not know how good it is. My father had many opportunities for getting in all the supplies that he wanted, as well as for making a good deal of money by exchanging his rice and salt for cotton, and then sending the cotton out by the blockade-runners to Nassau; but he was opposed to the running of the blockade for private gain…*

We had only one caddy of tea, which was kept for sickness, and a very little coffee. As a substitute, people used bits of dried sweet potato parched, and Indian corn parched, also the seed of the okra; this made a very rich drink, very full of oil. The root of the sassafras made a very nice tea. Sugar was very scarce, so mamma planted sorghum, a kind of sugar-cane which made very nice molasses, which Nelson boiled in the big copper kettle. I made delicious preserves with honey, and we dried figs, and mamma made all the vinegar we used with the fig-skins, put in a cask and fermented.

Confederate Receipt Book, published in 1863 by West & Johnston in Richmond, is now part of the Rare Book Collection at the University of North Carolina–Chapel Hill, and the recipes are designed as tips for citizens and soldiers to make nutritious dishes with few ingredients.

It details making pumpkin bread using only pumpkin and flour; how "To Raise Bread Without Yeast"; peas pudding made with split peas, egg, butter, salt and pepper; apple pie without apples; artificial oysters; a "Method of Curing Bad Butter"; how "To Judge the Quality of Lamb"; "Preserving Meat Without Salt"; and several rice recipes, including rice flour sponge cake.

A Cheap and Quick Pudding

From Confederate Receipt Book: A Compilation of Over One Hundred Receipts, Adapted to the Times *(electronic edition)*

Beat up four eggs, add a pint of milk and little salt, and stir in four large spoonfuls of flour, a little nutmeg and sugar to your taste. Beat it well, and pour it into buttered teacups, filling them rather more than half full. They will bake in a stove or Dutch oven in fifteen minutes.

Chapter 10
POSTBELLUM COOKERY

After the Civil War ended, Bessie Pringle tried to continue growing rice, as did many other plantation owners. However, the lack of a free labor force (slaves) and a series of devastating hurricanes between 1893 and 1911 that severely flooded and damaged fields effectively ended that era's large-scale rice production.

Bessie Pringle was an enterprising woman, however, and she eked out a living. She sold some property, and she made money writing a newspaper column about life on a rice plantation under the pseudonym Patience Pennington. Her book, *A Woman Rice Planter*, is a compilation of those letters with beautiful pen and ink illustrations by Alice Huger R. Smith.

Pringle wrote of growing crops and livestock, forging new relationships with former slaves and gathering nature's bounty. Seafood and freshwater fish were valued postwar foods, and she described how herring runs providing welcome spring feasts:

> *During the run of herring in the spring they crowd up the little streams in the most extraordinary way, just piling on top of each other in their haste to reach the very source of the stream, apparently. I suppose one little leader must wave its little tail and cry "excelsior" to the others. At a small bridge over a shallow creek near here a barrelful has been taken with a dip-net in an afternoon. But it takes a meditative, not to say an idle person, to watch for the special day and hour when the herring are seized by the impulse to ascend that particular stream.*

A WOMAN RICE PLANTER   375

"Miss Pashuns, if I neber eat rice again I won't eat rice Goliah cook! But den I'se bery scornful!"

Fanning and pounding rice for household use.

August 29.

Chloe and Patty went to the funeral "sarmint," and it was grand. The eulogies of the departed were satisfactory to all. They left in the buckboard at 10 o'clock and returned at dusk,

Alice Huger R. Smith provided illustrations for Elizabeth Allston Pringle's 1913 book, *A Woman Rice Planter*, which describes Georgetown County life following the Civil War. *General Research & Reference Division, Schomburg Center for Research in Black Culture, the New York Public Library, Astor, Lenox and Tilden Foundations.*

Pringle's home was also situated at a prime spot for shad fishing. She described how five or six men set nets near her house during the season, which runs from the middle of January through April. However, she had no luck netting them herself, and evidently they were expensive to buy because she said she could not afford to eat them unless she bought one or two when company came to dinner.

Cows were kept for milk and butter production, and they were also slaughtered for their meat, although much less often than hogs since it is hard to preserve beef in the humid coastal weather.

"If you have a cow calf, there's value to her since she can grow up and produce milk," said Walter Hill, director of the Horry County Museum. "A bull calf doesn't have that much value since one bull can service a lot of cows. So that bull calf is what they ate, when he gets up to enough size to butcher him but not be a second mouth to feed. Then you'd share the beef with your neighbor or extended family to get it eaten as quickly as possible before it went bad." Sheep were also commonly kept on farms for their meat and for their wool.

One food source that diminished after the Civil War was ricebirds. The tiny bobolinks were a problem during the height of rice plantations as they swarmed rice fields during spring sowing and just before fall harvest, and if they were not chased away by gunshot or the waving of arms or banging of pots, huge migrating flocks could seriously damage crops. However, the little birds were tasty, although it took a bit of work to clean enough for a meal. But after the rice fields waned, bobolinks moved their migration paths elsewhere.

I have sent to try and get some rice-birds for my dinner. These are the most delicious little morsels, so small one can easily eat six for breakfast, and a man makes nothing of a dozen for dinner. We used to get them in great abundance only a few years ago, but now the rice-bird industry has become so big a thing we find it very hard to get any at all. Formerly a planter hired bird minders, furnished powder and shot, and shot several dozen birds from each one; but now the negro men go at night with blazing torches into the old rice-fields, which are densely grown up in water-grasses and reeds, the birds are blinded and dazed by the light, and as the fat little bodies sway about on the slender growth upon which they rest, they are easily caught, their necks wrung, and they are thrust into the sack which each man has tied in front of him. In this way a man sometimes gets a bushel by the time the reddening dawn brings him home, and he finds waiting for him on

One solution to ricebirds that devoured rice crops was to catch and eat them. *Photo by David Watkins.*

the shore buyers form the nearest town, who are ready to pay thirty cents a dozen for the birds, so that one or two nights of this sport give as much as a month's labor.

Even in those lean times, the long growing season and abundance of wildlife and seafood in the Grand Strand area kept most people from going hungry. "Where I live," Bessie Pringle wrote, "there is no hunger, no want; life is so easy, food so plentiful. A few hours' work daily feeds a man and his family." Pringle described an event in 1904 when Jim, one of the men who worked for her, came across an elderly half-blind woman who hadn't eaten since the day before and was hungry:

> *"Oh," I said, "Jim, did you give her something to eat?"*
>
> *"I didn't have nothing to eat with me, ma'am, but the sticks of candy you giv me to take to my chillum; but I giv her them, en you never see any one so pleas." Then he went on to say: "It seems to me sence I ken remember this is the first person I ever seen real hungry."*
>
> *"You mean you have never met a hungry person on the road before?"*

"I never met none on the road nor never seen none nowhere that was perishin' with hunger."

Pringle said she was not surprised because her mother always sought to give food to those who needed it at Christmastime. However, she never learned of anyone who needed subsistence food, although there were many who welcomed gifts of sugar, coffee, tea and tobacco.

Pringle also described a family, a former slave named Old Maum Mary who lived with her husband, Old Tom. They had a "little farm of their own, where they plant a field of corn, a patch of rice, a patch of cotton, and one of tobacco. They raise three or four hogs every year and have a cow. In addition to these they have a most prolific pear tree and a very large scuppernong grapevine, and the sale of their fruit brings them in a nice little income."

Pear trees were extremely common in Grand Strand yards. "This country is the home of the pear," Pringle wrote. "Both the Keiffer and Le Conte grow and bear luxuriantly, and the pears reach immense size." Apples were not as abundant, but there were some apple trees. In October 1904, Pringle was thrilled to receive a gift from a neighbor of a dozen apples. "I was greatly touched by it," she said. "Such a great present here, where we see no fruit but pears."

As for scuppernong grapes, Pringle detailed making wine from them in September 1904. She got two and a half gallons of wine from ten quarts of grapes:

Every negro cottage through the long line of villages which fill the pine woods has at least one scuppernong vine, from which they sell bushels of grapes, besides eating them for a month. One vine will cover several hundred feet of space, for they are never trimmed, but grow laterally on scaffoldings made about five feet and a half from the ground.

They do not grow in bunches like other grapes, but only four or five very large grapes together, so that when you go under an arbor of ripe grapes you see no leaves above you, only a canopy of grapes, the leaves being all on top, and there is no more delicious experience than a half hour under a really old grape-vine in early September.

The older the vine the more luscious the grapes, and the perfume is most exquisite. It is a native of North Carolina, but takes kindly to this State and requires no spraying or care of any kind beyond breaking away the dead twigs and branches during the winter season—and mulching with dead leaves.

Sweet potatoes continued to be a favorite sustenance food. They grow well in the sandy coastal soil, they're extremely nutritious and after they're dried a bit to release a little moisture, they store well in potato banks with no other preservation methods required. Pringle planted 1.75 quarters acres of them in 1904, yielding almost two hundred bushels. That same fall, Pringle visited a widow whose garden contained turnips, cabbages, carrots, beets and tomatoes, and she had a milk cow. In October, Pringle was busy picking field peas and described her pea-picking apron: "It is made of light blue denim, quite long and turned up like a sewing apron only much larger, for it can hold nearly a bushel of peas." She also noted that field peas were selling for ten cents per quart.

"Mom Melia," shown here with a milk pan circa 1930, was a midwife from the Freewoods interviewed by Genevieve Willcox Chandler for the Works Project Administration's oral history project. *Photo by Bayard Wootten. Brookgreen Gardens Collection, Georgetown County Library, Georgetown, South Carolina.*

Beyond the abundance of foods for those who worked to grow or hunt it, a striking commonality of lean times among Grand Strand residents is the strong tendency for neighbors to care for one another. If one person had butterbeans and another had sweet potatoes, they traded one for the other. When someone was old and sick and had no family, a neighbor would cook for them. If so many fish were caught that one family couldn't eat or preserve them all, they willingly gave the extras to neighbors, knowing that the gift would be reciprocated at some point with honey or grits or pear butter.

A forty-acre living farm museum called Freewoods Farm re-creates "life on small Southern family farms owned and/or operated by African Americans between 1865–1900." It is located at 9515 Freewoods Road in the Burgess area of Myrtle Beach.

Chapter 11
EARLY TWENTIETH CENTURY

As the twentieth century began, times were still hard for Southerners recovering from the Civil War, and wealthy Northerners were able to buy inexpensive coastal winter retreats coveted for their wild game, peacefulness and beauty.

Bernard Baruch, a wealthy financier and statesman from New York who was an advisor to some of the world's wealthiest and most powerful people, including presidents, bought a hunting paradise. Between 1905 and 1907, he purchased 17,500 acres just north of Georgetown for about $3.15 per acre, according to Lee Brockington's book *Plantation Between the Waters: A Brief History of Hobcaw Barony*.

Winston Churchill visited in January 1932, arriving at the Hobcaw dock on his yacht. President Franklin D. Roosevelt visited for a month in 1944, and when he died in April 1945, "his doctors and his family felt that the month spent at Hobcaw literally added the year to his life."

But while President Roosevelt rested, many other visitors came for the hunting. When Baruch visited the site of Hobcaw Barony in 1904 and went duck hunting, "he felt it was some of the best ducking to be found anywhere," Brockington wrote. "The sky was black with waterfowl, and sixty-odd shells could bring down forty-five ducks. No bag limits existed at that time and no one knew when to stop. Baruch called it a veritable 'Shangri-La' and declared the land the most beautiful spot in the world."

In a personal interview, Lee Brockington discussed the dining habits of the Baruchs and other residents of Hobcaw Barony, which is now owned by

In a circa 1910 postcard made for guests, Annie Baruch (second from right) and Bernard Baruch (far right) pose with three hunters and one hundred ducks at Clambank Landing at Hobcaw Barony. *Belle W. Baruch Collection, Georgetown County Library, Georgetown, South Carolina.*

the Belle W. Baruch Foundation, established by Bernard Baruch's daughter, and has a public visitors' center. All 17,500 acres of it are intact, and site tours are regularly scheduled.

When Baruch purchased Hobcaw Barony, about three hundred African American slave descendants still lived on the property in former slave cabins. They were given the opportunity to remain there and work on the property if they wished.

Hobcaw Barony visitors hunted and fished with brothers Sawney, Ball, Pluty, Hucks and Bob Caines—local guides, outdoorsmen and artistic duck decoy carvers. Resident African Americans retrieved the ducks because much of the hunting took place in areas crusted with sharp oyster shells that would have injured retriever dogs' feet. No federal game limits were established until 1918, so until then, the Baruchs and their guests had self-imposed limits of one hundred ducks apiece per day. "One hundred-duck days," Brockington said. "How could they possibly eat that many ducks?"

Brockington knew from interviewing former African American residents who lived at Hobcaw that the ducks weren't given to them. In fact, hunting ducks, deer and wild turkeys was not allowed to them, although sometimes venison was shared and they could kill wild hogs. "[Ducks, turkeys and deer] were wild game that was reserved for the Baruchs and their guests," she said.

Brockington found an answer to the question of what was done with all those ducks in a 1922 letter from the Baruch archives. "It was from President Warren G. Harding," she said. "It said, 'Thank you Bernie for the smoked ducks from Hobcaw.'"

The smokehouse remains on Hobcaw property and was recently conserved, and Brockington noted that the hand-forged hooks on which meat once hung are still in place. "You can open the door and smell the breeze of ham and smoke and all those mixed smells," she said. "I love the idea they were smoking ducks and sending them up north to friends." By the 1930s, Brockington wrote, the numbers of ducks had declined dramatically.

In addition to ducks, turkeys and deer, the Baruchs ate terrapins, clams, oysters, fresh fish, sturgeon caviar and wild hogs. The Baruch kitchen housed an impressively sized fish poacher that Brockington said "would hold an entire fish." A pit for burning oak logs was maintained to create charcoal for roasting hogs. "They had all the hogs they could eat," Brockington said. "Most of the time when they did the barbecue, they did the true pit cook barbecue out on the yard or in the field when they were hunting. They would come up out of the boat or out of the field, and the barbecue would be ready."

Almost everything the Baruchs ate came from their property, which Brockington said Bernard and his wife, Annie Griffen Baruch, and their three children—Belle, Junior and Renee—occupied from Thanksgiving to Easter. They had gardens filled with peas, corn, French asparagus and other vegetables, and Brockington said that as an adult Belle Baruch had a large Victory Garden. The original Baruch residence and a new one completed in 1931 both had full bars, even during Prohibition.

Down at Friendfield Village—which was where many of the African American Hobcaw residents lived in a former slave village named for one of the fourteen rice plantations that became Hobcaw Barony—food was more modest. The cabins, which still stand today, have never had electricity or running water.

One male resident who lived in Friendfield Village as a child told Brockington that his mother started a pot of grits in the mornings and served that with a bit of leftovers and cornbread for breakfast. A school for black children was located on Hobcaw property, and he remembered taking peanut butter sandwiches and fried bread in his lunch pail. "And on a good day they had jelly," Brockington said. "A lot of people put up jelly. There were a lot of figs, mulberries and blackberries. There were a lot of pear trees in the area."

Recently, Grand Strand Master Gardeners re-created an "African Heritage Garden" on Hobcaw property. They planted pattypan squash, okra, red potatoes, white potatoes, field peas, cowpeas and beans. "Black-eyed peas weren't the biggest thing," Brockington said. "Cowpeas and field peas were the two big things."

The Georgetown and Pawleys Island areas had several truck farms and a cannery. In 1926, 150 refrigerator car loads of produce were shipped from the area, and commonly grown produce included corn, cowpeas, soybeans, Irish and sweet potatoes, peanuts, watermelons, sugar cane, oats and rye.

When the Lafayette Bridge (today called the L.H. Siau Bridge) in 1935 replaced ferries as the way for people to get to and from Georgetown over an expanse of water where the Pee Dee, Black and Waccamaw Rivers merge, dining habits of area residents changed.

"After 1935, when the bridge was built to the mainland, most [African American Hobcaw residents] abandoned gardening," Brockington said. "It was a whole lot easier to buy a can of beans for a few pennies… Transportation was provided once a week to Georgetown, and the stores in Georgetown stayed open until really late, until ten o'clock on payday. There were credit accounts—Mr. Baruch ran accounts for the aged and infirm on his plantation, and I do not doubt the Vanderbilts and the DuPonts and the other [wealthy landowners] did the same sort of arrangement in town." The completion of the Lafayette Bridge also brought more travelers through the Grand Strand area because it was the last link completing unfettered road travel on U.S. 17 between Maine and Miami.

The late Horry County historian Catherine Lewis grew up in the western Horry County town of Loris, which she wrote was "settled mostly by second- and third-generation Scots whose families had populated the Cape Fear region of North Carolina." The railroad went through there around 1887, and by 1900, the little town had a high school. The turpentine business gave way to tobacco farming.

"By the mid-1930s," she wrote, "Loris had a thousand residents. Jennings W. Hardwick, mayor, bragged in an address published in the *Horry Herald* (July 2, 1936), that fifty percent of South Carolina's tobacco crop grew within a twenty-five-mile radius of his town. Its four warehouses sold six millions pounds a year. Strawberries, beans, Irish potatoes, sweet potatoes, lettuce, and poultry were grown for northern markets."

In the 1930s, Lewis attended grammar school in Loris, and she remembered that students who lived in town brought for lunch peanut butter, mashed banana and peanut butter or pimento cheese sandwiches on store-bought bread, while those who lived in the country had ham and eggs on biscuits. During the Depression, the first school lunch program started, and Lewis said that the same food was served every day: vegetable soup, which cost each student a nickel for a large cup. Or, if the child didn't have a nickel, his or her parents sent in in fresh produce from the farm for the next day's soup pot.

Don Camlin and his sister, Becky Ward Curtis, remembered what it was like growing up in Georgetown. "Ducks were so plentiful in the '40s and '50s, it was unbelievable," Camlin said. "You could go hunt one hundred ducks any time you wanted to…At five o'clock, you'd see five hundred fly by, then another five hundred, then another five hundred. There was a 250-acre pond at Debordieu, and you couldn't even see the water for all the ducks."

Camlin and Curtis were lucky to have two parents who loved to cook. Their father, Wade O. "Buster" Camlin, and their mother, Cora Trudell "Dell" Williams Camlin, both cooked for their large country families while they were growing up. As adults, Buster Camlin was known as a barbecue pit master, and Dell Williams dazzled friends and family with her culinary skills. Curtis remembered:

My mother was one of the greatest cooks in the world. She cooked quail by browning it in the frying pan after she floured it and salted and peppered it. We have to have lots of pepper in our family. Then she made the gravy and put the quail back in the gravy. Daddy would put [parboiled] quail on the charcoal grill, and doves, and mop it with his barbecue sauce.

We had a big old screened back porch, and it was full of hams hanging, and sausage. I remember coming home from school one day, and there was a cow in our yard. Daddy had a Studebaker business, and someone owed him some money and couldn't pay him, so they went and got their cow and brought it to the house. Next thing I know we're having steak every day—steak and grits in the mornings for breakfast. I have never seen people cook as much food as my mom and dad in my life. We always had huge breakfasts with grits and redeye gravy and salt-cured ham.

Of course you had grits, you always had grits. [Mother] put a little cornmeal and flour in her grits. We would have eggs, lots of eggs, and she always made homemade bread.

Don Camlin added, "She made homemade bread right until the day she died."

"And when anybody came to her house, you always had something homemade cooked to offer them, and coffee was always ready," Curtis said. "You didn't walk in her house without having something homemade to eat."

Transportation Changed Everything

At the start of the twentieth century, beachgoers no longer had to rely solely on ferries or steamships to get them to the coast because railroad tracks finally crossed swamps and rivers west of the Grand Strand, and then automobiles began to be introduced.

A 2013 display at the South Carolina Maritime Museum in Georgetown shows that in 1905 the D.J. Crowley Company in Georgetown provided artificial ice and manufactured and bottled mineral soda waters, ginger ale, lager beer and sarsaparilla. R.Y. Cathou & Sons in Georgetown bought, sold and shipped seafood (especially smoked sturgeon and sturgeon caviar), as did several fish houses along the Sampit River that processed and shipped shrimp, oysters, menhaden, sturgeon, shad and more, which is a topic that can be delved into extensively at the Georgetown County Museum. Independent Seafood, established in 1939 on the Georgetown waterfront by Herbert Tarbox and V.C. Simpkins, is still in business as of 2013. Between 1900 and 1930, according to Dean Cain, writing in the 2008 *Winyah Bay Heritage Festival Guide*, several oyster canneries dotted the Grand Strand from Georgetown to Little River.

Land cleared by the lumber and naval store industries sprouted truck farms that shipped tons of produce to northern states. A 1915 photo in the Georgetown County Library Digital Archives shows a truck loaded with Georgetown County–grown cabbages ready for shipment.

L.C. Lachicotte owned the Cove Oyster Company at Waverly Mills and canned seafood as well as vegetables. "Lachicotte also operated a cannery at Huntington Marsh on the south end of Murrells Inlet," wrote Cain in his 2008 article. "He was most likely the first in South Carolina to actively cultivate oysters to replenish stocks and the first to grow oysters in brackish water ponds." The last cannery closed in the mid-1960s, according to Cain.

The first trains reached Loris and Conway in 1887, and in 1900, two trains started taking local industrial employees and their families on weekends to

Watermelon has long been a favorite cool summer treat in the Grand Strand area, as evidenced by this circa 1900–1915 group in Pawleys Island. *Georgetown County Library Photograph Collection, Georgetown County Library, Georgetown, South Carolina.*

Myrtle Beach. By 1902, Georgetown had two daily railroad mail deliveries. From 1901 to 1905, a train carried employees of the Atlantic Coast Lumber Company from Hagley Landing to Pawleys Island, until a hurricane destroyed the tracks and bridge. The railway was replaced by a road.

With a railroad came a hotel, and the Seaside Inn was built in Myrtle Beach in 1901. Boardinghouses serving food, as well as a few restaurants, began to feed hungry tourists throughout the Grand Strand area. In 1908, the first Myrtle Beach Pavilion was built.

Clay Nance can trace his family in Myrtle Beach to the late 1800s. His great-grandfather, Daniel Wayne Nance (1890–1965), was a commercial fisherman and community developer, and Myrtle Beach's Nance Plaza is named for Dan Nance and his wife, Ellen Todd Nance (1894–1967). Dan Nance's father was Marshall Homes Nance (1860–1944), and Clay has a clipping from a 1955 article that ran in the *Myrtle Beach News* in which Myrtle Beach resident Casper L. Benton (1897–1980) of general contracting firm C.L. Benton & Sons recalled that "Captain Marshall Nance had a sandwich stand where he sold cornbread fish sandwiches" around 1915. "They sold for about a nickel," the article quotes Benton as saying. "Nobody had a dime in those days."

The article also describes how

> *the railroad…came in close by the pavilion and continued on to the beach where it stopped near a small beach shelter. This railroad was an extension*

of the present railway [in 1955] *which now stops at the Atlantic Coastline Terminal. "The beach shed looked like a country depot and excursion trains from inland brought visitors to the beach,"* [Benton] *recalls. "Fish camps were located where the present amusement center lies. There was no law in those days. This arrival of the excursion trains usually resulted in free-for-alls between the natives and the visitors," Mr. Benton said. He tells how the natives met the train and, "picked fights with the newcomers."*

One of the trains was called the Black Maria. It brought visitors who enjoyed meals at boardinghouses, and Jack Bourne of Myrtle Beach has a photo depicting a hot dog stand selling "frankfurters," ice cream and candy as early as 1924. The Colonial Coffee Shop was at the intersection of East Broadway Street and Kings Highway in 1937, and Ye Olde Tavern was on the oceanfront where Ocean Front Grill, established in the mid-1950s, is currently located in 2013. The Atlantic Bread Company was on Ocean Boulevard in the spot that soon became Peaches Corner, which is still in business in 2013 and still sells foot-long hot dogs topped with mustard, chili and onion. At 819 Main Street was the Kozy Korner Tavern, flanked by Divines Fish Market and the Wonder Bar.

A circa 1920 photo in the Georgetown County Library Digital Archives shows a Front Street café in Georgetown, "where 'Miss Nettie' Gladstone served rice and duck every Saturday. The second and the third floors made of wood housed the guests." A pier and pavilion were in place on Pawleys Island by 1923, and in the 1930s, the Pawleys Island inn and restaurant The Beacon was serving three meals a day.

The 1920s were roaring at Davis' Dance Hall and Store in Pawleys Island. A caption under a photo of the business in *Pawleys Island: A Century of History and Photographs* notes that it was built in the late 1920s and was "open all night. Robert Quinn of Georgetown once wrote in 'South Carolina Magazine,' 'As night came on blood ran hotter, the revels became more carefree and those of faint heart or stern upbringing avoided the place. Davis' was the purveyor of the favorite local anesthetic, a brand of apple wine recommended for its economy not its smooth flavor or pleasant after-effects!'"

In 1930, the Ocean Forest Hotel opened in Myrtle Beach, and it was billed as the finest hotel resort in the mid-Atlantic. It had ballrooms, crystal chandeliers and a fine restaurant along with a golf course and country club, and it lured a new level of prosperous tourists to that part of the Grand Strand.

Chapter 12
THE GREAT DEPRESSION AND FARM LIFE BY THE MONTH

Wayne Skipper is uniquely qualified to inform others about life on Horry County farms before there was electricity and even cars, and he expounded on what these people ate and how they preserved food. He's the farm manager at the L.W. Paul Living History Farm north of Conway. Part of the Horry County Museum, the farm re-creates life in rural Horry County from 1900 to 1955.

Skipper was raised on a farm a few miles west of Conway, and his roots in the area go deep. His father, Ernest Walden Skipper (1929–2003), was a tobacco farmer, as was his grandfather, Jesse Grier Skipper (1900–1954). Beyond that, the Skipper roots can be traced to the early 1800s, all in Horry County.

"The Skippers on my grandfather's side was heavily Native American," he said, "as was my grandmother Cannon. They were Cherokee…The Native Americans were almost in the class as the minorities with the blacks in this time period, so they did not elaborate or talk about their ancestry."

His mother, Mary Dean Owens Skipper, was born in 1934, and her father was William Thomas Owens (1902–1972), married to Mamie Eulee Cannon. Their family is traceable to the early 1700s in Horry County.

My family had a cow; we milked year round. As long as you keep that cow milked on a regular basis, I've had people say they've milked a cow twelve years off of one calf being born. And so you continually have milk. And your cream. And your butter. I can't remember as a child growing up seeing a cow have a calf on a yearly basis.

After the Second War, electricity came along, and they could freeze things, and so my dad started raising a few beef cattle. Before we had a freezer in the home, the butcher shop had locker plants. There were lockers, or boxes, in there that you could rent. They'd process your beef for you there, and then they would actually keep it there frozen for you. Every time you went to town, you'd go by and get some of your fresh-frozen beef out of your locker. It cost you so much rent a month. But before electricity, there was very little beef consumed here.

We had electricity in the '40s around here, especially after the war. After 1945, it was complete throughout the rural area.

JANUARY

January, of course it being cold, the rule on the farm was the smokehouse was the center point of their food. In January, there wasn't many vegetables available that were fresh. The main one would have been collard greens. January would have been the peak of having collard greens for the food. There may have been some turnip roots. By this time, most of the green part would have been killed by the cold or died down.

On the meat side of things, of course this would have been the month, in relation to the butchering day, that their pork would have been in the salt. It takes two days for every pound, and that would have depended on the thickness. Normally there was a bench or a dugout log in the smokehouse. They would have packed that meat in salt, allowing as much airspace around it as possible. When it's touching, the moisture wants to rise from the bottom piece and can't get through to the second, so they need to be separated from each other.

Your moisture in the very beginning is going to drain. If it was in a dugout trough, they may put planks or slats down in it so when the meat began to drain, it would drain on down, then the moisture would evaporate on out. It wouldn't take long for it to stop the draining process. It's still going to absorb salt, but it will evaporate after the initial week or two.

Some were very particular about what side the skin was on. My grandfather, according to my father, always turned the skin down. Now, my father said he just never could understand doing that. The skin would hold the moisture in that draining process. If you had it turned up, the skin wasn't like a basin holding that moisture in there. Some was real picky about that, but my father always wanted to turn the skin up so that it could evaporate

Hog butchering was an eagerly anticipated event for Horry County residents hungry for fresh meat. *Photo circa 1930–50 by William Van Auken Greene. William Van Auken Greene Collection, Horry County Museum, Conway, South Carolina.*

faster. You're wanting to dry it as much as possible. That process is what they call "taking salt."

They may put more salt on it from the original rubbing. Putting salt on it, they called it "rubbing the salt in." They'd take their hand and rub it on the pork, and you'd see more moisture come to your hand just by rubbing it. And then they may do that again. It was according to how much time they had and how much salt they put on it to begin with. There are a lot of variations in and the reasons why they did things.

Bacon pieces didn't take long because they were thin. You may take them out and start a little smoke on them earlier. They wanted it to stay there until the salt until it penetrated to the bone.

At that time, they were probably eating more fresh meat from the butchering than at any other time of the year. Along with [that], they did some canning of fresh meat. The backbone part of the pork, they didn't do a lot of preserving of that with salt or smoking; it would have either been canned or ate up fresh at that time.

And, of course, there were sausages. If they stuffed them, they could hang them. They'd loop them over something like a tobacco stick—something they cleaned real good and could loop over it. They'd let it be drying, and when it got dry enough, they'd loop it through a lard stand. They'd melt fat or grease rendered from fat, pour it over the sausage and preserve it that way. The lard stand was tin material, with a tight-fitting cover on it. They had five-pound, ten-pound, twenty-pound, twenty-five-pound, depending how much space you had and how many you wanted to keep. Lard cans are still very much available today. You're not going to find them in a modern hardware store, but rural small towns will still carry them, or they can get them. After it was dried, they'd rope it because it was still attached by the casing, then pour melted lard on top of it to seal it over. Any time they wanted sausage, they'd use a spoon, pull up as much as they wanted to up out of it and cut it off.

I've read where they would actually take it and not put it in a casing. It was fresh like we know it today, and they'd put it in dry corn shucks and dry it that way and then put it in the lard stand and pour oil on it. They'd often refer to it as "oil sausage" because of the excess grease it was packed in. That was the canning part of the fresh meat they couldn't consume right away.

There was a government program, and they would go to a community where there was enough to participate. They weren't using jars; they used cans. My mother could remember the one in the community where she lived. There wasn't a town there, not a municipality. It was in the Pee Dee area, sometimes considered Dog Bluff. It ran from Aynor all the way out to Highway 701 south going toward Georgetown. That's the side of the county where the Little Pee Dee River traces the boundary. There was a schoolhouse called the Brownway schoolhouse; lot of folks in that area was named Brown. Her mother was a Cannon, and the small section in that area they would refer to a Cannontown. They set it up the cannery in the Brownway schoolhouse. You could take what food you had, and they would help you do the canning and seal it in metal cans. This was in the '40s, maybe late '30s. It was definitely before the Second World War.

Then you've got chicken basically every month because the family could consume the whole bird and there wasn't any preserving that had to be done. But there again they didn't want to consume a lot of those birds because they were very important—the hens were—for egg laying.

Some folks refer to fried chicken a lot. There wasn't a lot of fried chicken. If you're going to fry it, it needs to be pretty young because of the tenderness of it. There wasn't many small chickens hatched off by the hens in January. So if they're gonna eat chicken this time of year, most of the time it's going to be an older bird, and you couldn't fry it because it would be tough. So most of the time they would stew it, what we would call boil it today. It would go a little

Some Dutch ovens had concave lids so coals could be heaped on top. *Photo by Lincoln Rogers.*

From ground grits to hominy, corn was an important part of early coastal South Carolinians' diets. *Photo by Melvin Dyson.*

Left: Sweet potato pie, such as this one made by Jane Goings of Georgetown and served at Aunny's Country Kitchen, has been a local favorite dessert for hundreds of years. *Photo by Matt Silfer, Silfer Studios.*

Below: Hog maws are pig's stomach. After butchering, slaves were given the parts their masters didn't want. This slow-cooked recipe made by slave descendant Charles Johnson is served at Aunny's Country Kitchen in Georgetown. *Photo by Becky Billingsley.*

Opposite: Levon Hucks stirs chicken bog at the L.W. Paul Living History Farm near Conway. *Photo by Kurt Christiansen.*

Chicken bog can easily be made in quantities big enough to serve crowds. This recipe by Wayne Skipper, farm director at the L.W. Paul Living History Farm, can only be cooked in a tightly lidded cast-iron pot over an outdoor fire. *Photo by Kurt Christiansen.*

Cast-iron pork tenderloin is one of the gourmet farm-to-table dishes served at Vintage Twelve restaurant at Kingston Resorts, oceanfront in Myrtle Beach. *Kingston Resorts.*

Sweet potatoes helped fuel South Carolina Revolutionary War troops. *Photo by Nulinukas.*

Wayne Skipper, farm director at the Horry County Museum's L.W. Paul Living History Farm near Conway, demonstrates sausage making. *Photo by Becky Billingsley.*

Sweet potato banks at the L.W. Paul Living History Farm. *Photo by Kurt Christiansen.*

Left: Many Horry County families used corncobs in their smokehouses. *Photo by Kurt Christiansen at the L.W. Paul Living History Farm.*

Below: Marion Haynes, a technical assistant at the Horry County Museum, holds a pan of fried pork and biscuits at the L.W. Paul Living History Farm. *Photo by Kurt Christiansen.*

Levon Hucks plows the field, with help from Nell, at the L.W. Paul Living History Farm. *Photo by Kurt Christiansen.*

Preserving garden produce was hot but necessary summer work so food would last through the winter. *Photo by Becky Billingsley.*

Left: Fresh green boiled peanuts are an anticipated end-of-summer treat. *Photo by Matt Silfer, Silfer Studios.*

Below: Russell Vereen still makes the shrimp salad that was served at the Wayside; it calls for cottage cheese. *Russell Vereen.*

Hardened rosin left over from the days when the naval store industry boomed in the Grand Strand area was recovered from river bottoms by Jon Leithiser. He boils the sap to cook sweet potatoes. *Photo by Matt Silfer, Silfer Studios.*

Pinesap sweet potatoes are removed from the boiling sap with tongs and slid into paper bags. The hardened rosin crust, which is not eaten, keeps the potatoes warm for several hours. *Photo by Matt Silfer, Silfer Studios.*

Jon Leithiser, a Myrtle Beach native, continues the eighteenth-century local cooking tradition of boiling potatoes in pine rosin. *Photo by Matt Silfer, Silfer Studios.*

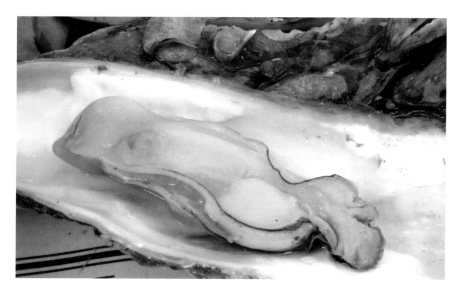

Intertidal cluster oysters harvested in the Grand Strand area are sweetly briny. *Photo by Becky Billingsley.*

Oyster roasts are a favorite type of outdoor coastal dinner party. *Photo by Matt Silfer, Silfer Studios.*

Left: Freshwater Fish Company near Conway serves fish and grits. *Photo by Matt Silfer, Silfer Studios.*

Below: Shrimp and grits is a specialty of the house at the River Room Restaurant, which is by the waterfront in Georgetown. *Photo by Keith Jacobs.*

Opposite, top: Lump crab cakes is one of the fresh local seafood recipes served at WaterScapes Restaurant at the Marina Inn at Grande Dunes in Myrtle Beach. *Photo by Becky Billingsley.*

Opposite, bottom: Collards and Mr. Nathaniel Green's cornbread muffins are served at Aunny's Country Kitchen in Georgetown. *Photo by Matt Silfer, Silfer Studios.*

Above: Catfish stew over rice is on the menu at Freshwater Fish Company north of Conway. *Photo by Becky Billingsley.*

Left: Traditional holiday fruitcakes in Horry and Georgetown Counties, such as this one baked by La-Ruth Jordan, are dense and moist. *Photo by Matt Silfer, Silfer Studios.*

farther that way because you could put other things with it like chicken and dumplings, chicken and noodles—that would be pastry to them—and they'd make it themselves. Put cornbread and stuff like that with it, and it would feed a larger number of people than just frying and cooking up a chicken, and of course a fry bird would have been smaller. Genes had not been changed to cause that fast-growing bird like we have today for fried chicken.

January was a pretty heavy month for fish. A fish called—the local term would have been mudfish. The wildlife department calls it a blackfish. It's a bottom feeder similar to a catfish, but mudfish has scales, and catfish doesn't. They would feed on the bottom in the mud. In January, you can start catching them in a net; they start running. The main reason for folks eating them [in] cold weather was the texture of the fish is a lot firmer. When it gets warm, especially when it gets hot, they get real soft and mushy. They didn't eat them like that.

Of course, they fry mudfish, cut them up in strips maybe the size of your finger and fry them. One of the most popular ways to cook them was what they called fish stew. They would categorize the type of stew by the color of it. They would say, "We're going to have fish stew, you going to do a red one or a white one?" And the red one was always tomato—some type of tomato cooked in the stew. It always had onions, and some may put potatoes in it when fish was about done.

My father would not eat it. He was born and raised right beside the river at the Waccamaw, and he could not tolerate the little bit of a taste of that fish being a bottom feeder in the mud because he was around that as a child, and of course when the water would rise and fall and it begins to evaporate, you get a scent of that in the air right there at the river. And that taste in relation to that—he didn't have any desire for mudfish stew.

But my mother was from a different river, the Little Pee Dee, and it has a sandy bottom, where the Waccamaw is pretty muddy, even though they look the same. The fish, they'd rather have them out of the Little Pee Dee because they didn't have quite [the] same type of river. My mother, she would cook white stew because that's what she liked.

Of course, they would use the head, the whole body of the fish. They didn't scale it like we would pan fish that we might catch from the river or even from the surf in the ocean. They would actually take a knife and sort of skin it, cross-sawing with a knife, with the knife in a horizontal position, and take the skin and those scales all at one time. They were slicing the scales off.

When she opened the cavity of the stomach and all, she would be careful to save the liver of the fish. On the intestines there would be yellow fat, and she would take all that off and save it. Take that and maybe stir-fry it, we would call it today, to extract the oil from that fat. And along with the onions, she'd put that in a pot and stew that fish with that liver and fat, and that would be called white stew. It would almost have a yellow tint to it, a yellow buttery color because the fat was that color. But they simply said red or white to distinguish from tomato base and not.

There was never filleting. Filleting fish as a child, I never heard of it. You used to didn't do that. The value of the food was too valuable to throw any part of it away. I learned as a child very early to eat fish and pick out the bones. They'd serve it with cornbread.

Rice was pretty special, but if they had it, they would serve rice with mudfish stew. Our part of the state wasn't in the rice-growing area. You get farther upland, they still don't eat rice in South Carolina. It comes from the tradition of being readily available. When you did get rice, it was not like we know it today, hull-less in a bag. It likely would still have the hull on it; they'd get it from a plantation growing rice, and they would husk it themselves. It would have a darker color to it because they didn't have the means of cleaning it that industry does today to make it white. They would beat it to get the husk loose with a mortar and pestle—a hollowed-out piece of hard wood and the part you beat with—and then they would have winnowed it.

They might not have had a winnowing basket on these small inland farms. They may just have had whatever basket. That winnowing basket makes it easy to toss it and catch it. But just hold it up out of a normal basket or tub as high as you can and catch the wind blowing and let it fall on a clean piece of burlap, sheet or tarp or whatever and let the wind winnow it that way.

Sunday meals were special always. That's where the most effort was put. If they had rice, it would be only on Sunday. But these mudfish were readily available in January, and I don't remember hearing anybody talking about preserving them.

They hunted wild game—squirrel, raccoon, opossum. The deer population in the time period of the history farm was sort of congregated to river bottoms; there were not a lot of upland game on high ridges on farmland. I guess from colonial days and Civil War years they depleted the population because there were no regulations between the harvest of male and female. There wasn't a real big comeback in the herds until the '60s and '70s when they began to repopulate.

But there were a lot of squirrel, raccoon and 'possum everywhere. I never heard much of folks eating bears in this part of the county, but I'm sure

Girls on Sandy Island, circa 1930, pour rice from a hand-coiled fanner or winnowing basket into a rice mortar. *Photo by Bayard Wootten. Brookgreen Gardens Collection, Georgetown County Library, Georgetown, South Carolina.*

they did. And they referred to them as hog bears because they were small black bears. They loved to attack pigs and kill them and eat them, so they called them hog bears. But that population was not real abundant in that time period. There's still a few of those still around today.

The wild turkey population was very sparse in that time due to overhunting. There was revitalization, conservation, really reintroducing that bird back into the wild and protecting them. We have just recently got a season where you can harvest wild turkeys again, and you have to harvest them by sex—you can't just kill either sex now. So there was very little wild turkey.

FEBRUARY

The collards are still abundant. Even if you get some warm days, and they're starting to get a seed head, that would have been the most popular green. They still have cornmeal and grits and sweet potatoes. They had a potato bank where they stored them. That would have been the most common carbohydrate. They have cane syrup, that's their sweetener; it's always on the table year round.

The difference between cane syrup and molasses is going to depend on who you're talking with. There is no difference. Most people that calls it molasses, they're referring to a different region where they could not grow sugar cane and they would grow sorghum cane. Sorghum cane will produce a seed head within a short growing season. Sugar cane does not produce a seed head until about sixteen months of a growing season. The sugar cane's going to be a little bit milder in flavor, but the consistency and the texture of it is going to be the very same. It's just a different variety of a plant. Now they could grow sorghum cane here, but not much of it's grown because most of the time the taste of sugar cane syrup is milder and a little sweeter than sorghum. But in regions where they can only grow sorghum cane, most of the time they're going to call it molasses.

I can remember the time my dad had a patch of cane up until I was ten or eleven years old. It began to get hard to find a place to process and syrup it. He never had the equipment, the pots and the kettles and all, to do that himself. So that was one reason it began to dwindle. When you could buy it from the grocery store, it was basically the same taste.

February is another season for fishing that was very popular, and that was for shad on the coast. Now that's a saltwater fish that comes up in the freshwater rivers and streams to spawn, and they do that in the wintertime. It starts in the middle of February.

These fish were netted; in the Big Pee Dee and the coastal section of the Waccamaw, they could catch them abundantly. Now this is a very strong-tasting fish, a very bony fish. My family would cook it with no breading whatsoever and a lot of salt and ground black pepper. They fried it in very hot oil or lard deep enough to deep-fry it. That helps extract some of that taste that's real fishy. If you bread it, it holds that taste. Salt it heavy, but if you salt it heavy you need hot grease. They would fry it pretty brown.

This fish is pretty thin and flat. They would cut it up and split it, not fillet it. The thickest part would have three splits. Fry it pretty brown, maybe a mahogany, like a syrup color. That also dries it out enough that you can even chew the bones. Folks would tell me they'd dice it in pieces about the size of your finger, which also frying it that way would allow the bones to cook enough you wouldn't have to extract them.

I really like shad. My family, we really like them, and I remember my dad fishing for them. Some of the folks couldn't afford to have a net, others used a bow net or a drift net that could actually drift with the flow of the water. The shad would come in small schools, and when the fish hit that net, they would immediately take them out because these fish will die very quick—they would drown. So they didn't set it and leave it; they would actually stay with it.

There were certain sections of the river according to the flow and the terrain or the curves and stuff in the river, the coves. They had learned that if you could set a net there and not have to drift, it was a good set. They would try to get that set every year because they knew they could catch fish right at that section according to the way the current was, and the fish went in the upstream trying to find a place to spawn.

I never heard of them preserving shad like pickling them or anything. They'd distribute them through their community, and they'd be fresh and fried. I never heard of cooking them any other way. Those were very popular in February and March.

You've got grits and meal and flour year round, sweet potatoes and all that. The chickens, of course, for stewing—those are things that stand out in my mind for February, along with your wild game and all.

MARCH

You're probably going to have some scallions or the green onion part that has started to grow. And you've got your tops of your onion. They would have dishes they would enhance with both parts of these new onions. Things like chopping the tops of onions and put it in their scrambled eggs, trying to enhance and break the norm of regular dishes.

Collards are still trying to make seed, and they're breaking off those lower leaves. And this would have been the time they would have started planting their cole vegetables. This is the cabbage family, [and] collards is a very popular part of the cole family. We know a lot today about broccoli, cauliflower and Brussels sprouts, but that was not very familiar to me. Cabbage was; that was a mainstay. You wanted to get those out because they're not going to tolerate our hot climate. And so they would have those planted. If need be, they'd even start to harvest that plant at the end of the month before it even began to head for a different flavor in the greens.

Of course there's sowing in early March. In middle to late March, they might start having turnip greens and not produce a root yet, but the green part itself along with mustard greens are the two greens I'm familiar with.

Then you've got three of the most popular varieties of turnips that were here. One was rutabagas. The rutabagas I'm familiar with are going to have an orange color to them. You've also got purple-tops. The globe of the plant itself is going be mostly white, and right around the top of it it's going to have a purple color to it. If you cut it open, it's all white on the inside. The green parts are going to have a little different texture: the rutabaga leaf is going to be more smooth than the purple-top leaf. A lot of folks like white egg turnips, which has a little bit of a bitter flavor, and they like that taste. Those are the main three varieties I'm familiar with. And of course, they all produce greens before they produce fruits.

In March, cabbage was steamed, seasoned with pork fat, fatback or the bacon or side meat, or a piece of ham or whatever. In late February and March, it became smoking time. The meat had absorbed enough salt in the smokehouse that they could begin hanging it and smoking it. That process has different recipes.

My family, especially on my mother's side, would wash that salt off from it being absorbed and drying. They'd clean the exterior piece real good, and they would make a basting to put on it. They would use syrup, more salt and borax. You could buy it; you can still buy it. It was called 20 Mule Team; I think that was just a brand name of borax. You make a paste with that. Paste it on, and it's going to be sort of grainy from the salt, and use the syrup and use enough water so you could spray it or smear it with your hand. They would smear that or spray it all over the outsides of those pieces of meat and hams, shoulders, the sides, bacon sides and put it in the smokehouse and begin to smoke it.

The wood they wanted to use for smoking would have been hickory, and a lot of times we think that they used it green. The smoking process is to extract more moisture, preserving it, along with sealing the outside. It's also enhancing the flavor a little bit. That basting along with the smoke would give it a golden brown color on the outside.

So that was mainly between at least February 15 and on into March. They would smoke a cold smoke for approximately seven days. Now this didn't go on twenty-four hours a day. The smokehouse was in the farmyard, and anybody that was old enough to be responsible enough to know what they were doing, as they went about their farm chores, they would stop and take a look inside.

Now, if they didn't have hickory, they could have used oak wood or fruitwood, but my family used corncobs. Corncobs will not burn readily if they're not real hot—they'll smolder. And they were abundant because they grew corn. If it began to flame up, they would take sand or water and spray on it to keep it from flaming and just smoldering in a cold smoke. All day long, they'd just keep checking and doing that, and basically do it six days a week because they weren't going to be smoking meat on Sundays because that was the Sabbath, and everyone was going to church.

And you've got sweet potatoes and your cornmeal and your grits and your flour for your carbohydrates, and that's going to continue year round. This is also the time to set out your sweet potato vines for the next fall's harvest.

When it comes to wild game in March, you're getting to the time when they stopped hunting because the reproduction of the small game, the breeding season, is coming. Perhaps the females have conceived at this time, and they respected them enough to not harvest them if they weren't in a dire need of meat, so that the animals could reproduce.

Flat fish, the pan fish, brim—there were several different varieties of brim here in the rivers. Then you've got other pan fish called hardheads, momouths, wallmouths, and they would begin to feed a little bit because your river temperature was going to change. They wouldn't be up in shallow water yet, but they knew from fishing the deep holes and their experience they would begin to bite a bait. So they began fishing before the fish began to rise because of the water temperature. They're going to be down in the deep holes for warmth—it protects them from the cold. There may still be some shad running too.

This is the time of year that you're trying to get a hen to take a nest. Before chickens were domesticated and were in the wild, spring is a natural time for them to set on eggs, and of course, that small chick will grow faster in the springtime because it's not getting real hot. They will hatch off right through hot weather, but it's hard on those small birds when it gets extremely hot. The earlier you get them hatched off, in March or April was the ideal month. But if a hen starts to get broody in March, they wanted her to go ahead and start.

According to how cold it was, whether the groundhog has seen his shadow or not, they would have planted garden peas or snow peas or English peas—we called them garden peas—over in January. They could have been coming up now and might have started to form a little hull, and they would cook the whole hull before the pea itself had matured inside of it. They would have probably had a pretty early spring to get any of those in March—it would have been late, late March.

My dad was very conservative about quail trapping in March and April because he wanted them to reproduce. You could catch them in a trap with corn as bait. The trap would set right on the ground; it was made out of chicken wire or biddy wire, very small mesh, thin-gauge wire. He could actually build that thing so that bird would go in and never come out.

That bird, when he goes in, he'll have his head down on the ground following the bait, and [my dad] would have a throat in it, or an opening that extended into the body of the trap, and the quail would go down through that harvesting the grain. Once he ate all that grain in there, of course he's an animal of flight—his head rises for escape. That throat (like a tunnel) is down there low. And so he's going around the pen with his head always up—he'll never stick it down and go out of that throat. The bird was not harmed in any way—the trap didn't pinch him or anything like that. We had an opening we could take loose where we had sewed it with more wire and reach our hand in and of course kill the bird.

The quail population has really dwindled now. The time period here [at the Living History Farm], the native quail—the bobwhite—was pretty abundant, but here it is almost extinct now, as far as the wild coveys. They were very abundant on the farm I lived on as a child in the '60s, just outside of Conway. It was called Four Mile because at that time we were four miles outside the city limits.

These farmers were not hunting for sport. They were hunting for food. My father didn't waste quail; we ate them. I never remember him trapping enough of those because he always looked out so they could repopulate. He never was much of a sport hunter; he mostly hunted for food. Fishing also; food was the main reason behind it. It wasn't just catch and release; it was too valuable.

APRIL

By this time, your meat is smoking in the smokehouse, so the mainstay of meat is going to return to that smokehouse. Most of the fresh pork is going to be gone unless it was canned, and your meat in the smokehouse is going to be done, so they're going to turn to that.

And, of course, there's chicken. The older birds that are not producing are what they're going to try to harvest. Very seldom is a hen going to hatch off little ones in March, but in April, this is going to start taking its flow when hens start to set. They knew from their flock who was going to be the best mothers, and they would have wanted them to set and try to break up those that were trying to be broody that they knew had a past of not taking care of their babies.

Sometimes a bunch of them would go broody, and they didn't need that many hatched off, and they would stop them from going broody. They would

Laying hens were too valuable for their egg production to use them as frying chickens. *Photo circa 1930–50 by William Van Auken Greene. William Van Auken Greene Collection, Horry County Museum, Conway, South Carolina.*

do that by taking that hen off that nest and sticking her in a bucket or a pail of cold water. The hen's body heat begins to rise; that's what puts her in that stage of sitting on eggs. And to stop that, they would just souse her in cold water, not to drown her, but to hold her in there a minute to drop that body temperature. They might have to do it several days in a row if she's trying to get back on her nest and set again. That's where you get the term "mad as a wet setting hen."

The young males you could tell by the size of their comb, that's where fried chicken comes in. Now those birds would have been real small. Some folks told me the drumstick, the leg, might not have been much bigger than a man's thumb. They didn't want all these male chickens running around because they were fighting and all that; they still had that gaminess in them even though they were not a game breed. There's enough of that instinct still there to become pretty aggressive. They would only save the males that the confirmation of their body was the ones they felt would be the best to reproduce from. They would begin to harvest those and begin to have fried chicken from the cockerels, or the males, while they were still young because they're tender enough that you can fry them. The hens were too valuable for their eggs to fry them.

In April, there was an abundance of your greens, turnip greens, mustard greens. Cabbage is going to start heading up. They're going to have steamed cabbage, and if there was an abundance of it, they may try to make some kraut. But kraut is hard to produce here in the spring because it gets very hot in the summertime, and if you don't eat it up before it starts getting hot, many times it will go bad and sour. More kraut making, of what was done here, was in the fall, where you've got a season of cole vegetables.

There's an abundance of turnip greens and mustard greens, which are of course producing roots by this time. The garden peas are going to be producing in April. Then your onions are really coming on good. Radishes would have been available.

And of course back to your cornmeal and your grits and your flour and sweet potatoes—things that was always there.

Of course, April was the planting month. Setting out and transplanting their tomato plants, planting all their beans, their field peas, their squash. If there was a tomato variety that was handed down and they really liked that variety, they could save the seed, take them from the fruit itself and let them dry. They would have to start those seeds in late December and January on the tobacco bed, where they had their tobacco transplants. Otherwise, they wouldn't have had enough time to start from seed. They'd also save pepper seeds. I can remember tomato and peppers in a little section cut out in the tobacco bed.

Corn was planted mostly in April, sometimes in March. They planted it later than today because it was very wet. There's a lot of drainage today to get the top water away. At that time, there wasn't a lot of drainage in the Lowcountry, and it was very wet. They were concerned more about too much water than they were not enough in the earlier part of the twentieth century. I can remember my dad doing a lot of ditching with the shovel, just in the field, to get a lot of top water off.

I can remember seeing Highway 501 between Conway and Aynor right at that four-mile section where it was two-lane, water running across it. Pretty common. And then a lot of times the rivers this time of year they would call a "fresh." The water would be high. That's when it would cross low-lying areas and some of the roads because there's not a lot of canals and ditches dug at that time.

And it's a very wet county too. It's hard to imagine sometimes how wet this place was. I can remember the farm we lived on when they got some heavy equipment in and started to dig some bigger-sized canals. This would have been in the '60s. Before then, they were more concerned about getting water away than they were about not having enough. So they would plant corn later, and the varieties were later, because they had more moisture.

We had a pretty big vegetable garden. Some of my parents' family was not on a farm, and they would help us sometimes. This is after the Second World War. A lot of folks were being able to work public jobs, paying jobs, getting off of the farm after the war because that was more available. The vegetable garden before the Second World War would have been pretty large, too, because they were depending on that for their food, due to not having a lot of income to actually buy food.

Ours was maybe an acre at the most. I'm not including things like watermelon or sweet potatoes or peanuts. I'm talking about just the vegetables of beans, spring peas, garden peas, your Irish potatoes. Those sweet potatoes and watermelons were a large enough crop they wouldn't have been included in the vegetable garden. Nor would the sugar cane have been included in that.

Also in April, they were able to start harvesting some Irish potatoes, or white potatoes. They would have been planted if at all possible in February. And so you're going to start getting small ones coming on that plant the size of maybe golf balls. They would not take up the whole plant; they would go "grabbling taters." That was just going with your hands around that plant, and you could feel them. I guess the correct term would have been "graveling," but they said "grabbling." They were getting their hands in the soil and feeling for those little potatoes that had begun to produce on that plant. They would pick those off without destroying the plant, then pack the dirt back up around it.

These potatoes at this time of year were very good, very fresh. The skin or peel was very thin on them. They would cook those in lots of ways. One I recall, we called them stewed potatoes. They would cook them in water with onions and some of that smoked seasoned meat from the smokehouse, with very little water. They would put dumplings in just before the water dropped off of the potatoes in the pot and would make cornbread dumplings or flour bread dumplings. They'd lay them down in the pot, and by the time the water got off, it had steamed them.

They would put them together with those garden peas, those potatoes, and their taste was just a sign of spring. My grandfather, I don't remember my grandfather, but my dad always said he said, "Don't never eat new potatoes and go to sleep at night, because if you die in your sleep you'll die hungry." If you've ever experienced and eaten those potatoes at night, the next morning you'll wake up hungry. I guess it's because they just digest so easily.

When they're the best is after you got some left from the supper meal the night before, and they've sat there and got cold overnight. And the next morning? Oh my. There is just nothing like cold new potatoes. They've just had time to mellow and absorb all the flavors and everything, and I can hurt myself on them. New potatoes the next morning, especially with a hot piece of cornbread, some bacon, some fresh ham or something or another was the best.

They didn't waste anything. Even if food was to spoil, it wasn't wasted; it went back to those animals. They realized the value of it.

MAY

There was a few crops would be planted in May. Cotton, if they wanted to grow cotton, it had to be planted in May. Okra is something that's sort of like cotton; it even looks like cotton planted in the field. It's small. They say don't plant okra or don't plant cotton until you have to take your coat off in the morning time. Because what they were saying is that it has to be warm enough. It can't stand that cool night and will wilt right down and will die.

The Irish potatoes are really there now. They're not going to harvest the whole plant in May, but if you planted green beans in late March or early April, you're probably getting some small ones now, then you'd cook you those along with those small potatoes. It was very special.

In April, and May especially, you go back to fishing. In May, there was a fly that would fall on the river, called a mayfly. Those fish would feed on those. They would always tell me that when those mayflies start falling, you could forget your bait. You could tell everywhere there were fish, because they'd come up and feed.

But then again, the fish are starting to come shallower. Some of those pan fish like hardheads would start to spawn because the water was flowing, and that hard-flowing water, it would be shallow. And so it may be flowing out of the bank where the normal bank was, and then where a stream would break off from the main source of the river or come into the river was that hard-flowing water where there were hardheads.

Hardheads is what we called them, but some people called them stump knockers. The nose on them in relation to the normal flatfish—pan fish, brim and stuff—was almost blunt. It looked like it run into a stump and mashed its nose in. They called them hardheads because that head was pretty hard too. It had a bone right there in front where it was sort of blunted off.

When they would bite, it was very aggressive on the bait. It would just *bam*—slam into it. You could catch them spawning in shallow water; they were running very hard because the water was up high. You had to fish with a little short line, not over twelve inches, maybe from six to twelve inches. When you would stick it over in a stump hole or around the tree roots or very thick vegetation, down next to the water, it would be sort of wood and stem because it hadn't already started to sprout out.

But you could get your line in there, and by the time that bait went in the water, *pow*! He'd hit it, and hit real hard. I've even seen them hit so hard they'd come out of the water because of that short line and that force—they were running to it and grabbing it. There were just going to consume it and go. So we called them hardheads or stump knockers. I can remember when they were pretty abundant. Now today, I don't see a lot of them. Some of the old fishermen said they don't know what happened. They're just not there like they were. But even in the '60s and '70s, we could catch them.

Here's another term I heard my dad say. You've heard the old saying, "April showers bring May flowers." Things were really starting to bloom out and come forth now. Well, the fish are doing the same thing. That draw was there for that farmer to go fishing, go fishing, go fishing, go fishing, go fishing, and he might skip his plowing a day to go fishing. Well we'd ride by the farm, and my daddy would say, "That's fishing grass." It's just starting to come up, and you could see a little green tint across the field. He said it was fishing grass because the farmer should have already plowed, but he didn't plow—he went fishing. So he called it fishing grass. And he said, "Fishing grass will get you in trouble." It'll get ahead of you, and you won't be able to get it plowed because once that grass grew so tall, you needed to plow, you needed to cultivate. If you plow with a mule, and the grass gets up there with much size, you'll never kill it.

Your Irish potatoes, your garden peas, your green beans, your string beans as we called them are very abundant now. Still possibly you've got a pretty good size of your turnip roots now. Might not have very many greens because they would start to go to seed. Collards that had gone to seed and the leaves had begun to dry down, right in the bottom part of the stalk where that leaf was, you might have broke those old dead leaves away to feed them to your chickens or your hogs. But where that leaf was broke off, they'd start sprouting, and they would harvest those collard sprouts. They was trying to produce a seed head, but they were low enough on the collard plant to where the sun didn't hit it, and they hadn't seeded out and made a stem for seeds. So they'd go over there and pick off them collard sprouts. And they were very tender, very good, because they were young coming off that stalk.

Huckleberries, they got them in the woods. When the husband went fishing, the wife and children might have gone to the woods and went huckleberry hunting in the spring there, probably more so in late April and May. There wasn't a lot of strawberries grown here. Our climate doesn't handle strawberries real well. Some folks had a strawberry bed, and if you had them, May is your strawberry month. But there were wild strawberries here—a lot smaller than the strawberries today. They would have been in the woods, but they weren't abundant enough to harvest and preserve. They'd just eat them fresh, with cream, sugar on them, things like that.

JUNE

Your Irish potatoes, if you don't get them out of the soil before full moon in June, they're going to start rotting in the ground. It was a rush there to when the moon was low, after full moon in May, before it started the new moon, that last quarter of the shrinking moon, was to harvest the Irish potatoes. A potato left in the ground after then is going to start to decay. Even if you harvest them after that and they haven't started to decay, you can't hardly keep them. They plowed them up because they were trying to get it done. They'd go out there with a mule or tractor and what we called a middle buster. It was a big plow that would turn both ways and bust 'em out, and you'd go out and pick them up. Officially, if you'd look in the literature, they'd call that a lister plow. But folks around here called it a middle buster.

Of course, you've still got an abundance of green beans, or string beans. Most of the time, garden peas will be too tough. Your onion tops are starting to not be green. You're possibly going to have some cucumbers. They would have been eaten fresh and small. You wouldn't have started pickling yet because they were fresh and you hadn't had them. You'll have an abundance of cabbage in June. By July, the heads are going to start to burst or make seed. These cole vegetables are about going to be over in June, so you've got to get them harvested and preserve them in some way.

Of course, you're going to have some radishes, and they're going to start to seed up, and they're going to be overabundant. I've never heard of anybody cooking a radish or even preserving them. They're just a salad-type vegetable dish; maybe soak them in vinegar. If you planted beets, it's going to be time to harvest beets in June. If they go to July, they're going to be tough. Late June, if you've got your squash in, you're going to have squash in the latter part of that month.

Field peas, and there's a little difference between those and cowpeas, you want to start planting them in dark nights in June. The darks nights was when the moon was decreasing after the full moon, into the new moon, most of the time on the last quarter. You didn't plant during the night, just when you couldn't see the moon. The theory was that if you planted when the moon was down, the fruit would grow on top of the plant. So when you went to pick them, they weren't down in the bush. They were all over the top, and they were easy to pick.

By this time, all those cockerels, or those males that were hatched off, are going to be butchered, and there's going to be an abundance of fried chicken. You're going to hear a lot of people refer to wringing their necks. My dad did not believe in wringing chickens' necks. He'd chop the head off with a hatchet or a small axe. His reason for that: it gave the heart long enough time before it quit pumping to pump that blood away from that carcass.

If you wrang a chicken's neck, he's going to start flopping. If he hits something solid like a piece of wood or the side of a building or something, he could bruise, and you'd get a dark spot in the meat because the blood cannot come out. So my dad would very suddenly cut the bird's head off. You caught that bird and you're holding him in your hand if you're going to wring his neck, and you're got to twist him and to me he's going through that turmoil until that neck breaks. With a sudden chop, all the sudden it's all over. To me, it's more humane. Of course, that animal was going to flop and flutter. I've seen the blood actually spray from that cut from taking the head off. If you turn him loose and he's going to be jumping, you're going to get blood spray everywhere.

So [my dad] would have a basket there—an older basket that he wasn't going to use for anything else. He'd have it turned upside down with its feet in one hand. As soon as he cut that bird's head off, he picked up the bird and put him under that basket and held the basket down. That way he's not flopping all over the yard making a scene and blood spraying everywhere and not getting dirt up all around that cut. We had a lot brighter and prettier meat that way.

July

When you get into July, it's getting pretty hot. There's not a lot of fishing going on in July; the water's getting pretty hot. Some of those fish would start to bed so they could spawn. They would always look for that on the full moon in July. They may go brim fishing on the full moon, but that would have been basically the fishing in July. They could always go fishing as a whole, but with the spring growth of them eating the mayflies and going to bed and spawning, they're not going to bite real heartily in July.

In July, the fish may be more so going to try and get that bait out of their area. If they can't fan it away with their tail, they may actually attack it with their mouth, not to eat it but to actually move it away from that bed where they're going to spawn. So if they catch 'em on the bed, they're going to catch 'em by aggravation, by them being aggravated more than actually taking the bait.

There's no wild game at this time.

Now here your vegetable garden is really going to come off in July. All your beans and peas are going to bear. Your tomatoes are going to come off. Cucumbers are coming off, and there's your time if you're going to do some pickling, you gotta get it done because after July, the cucumbers are not going to produce any longer. Your okra's going to start small in late July. You want to pick it when it's small, finger-size. Any bigger than that, it is too tough. There is an abundance of being able to cook those daily greens for your meals, along with getting them canned.

As a child, I wasn't familiar with zucchinis. It was always yellow squash, summer squash we called it.

There may have been some apples in late June. The main fruits we're familiar with today started coming on in late June and the first of July, like apples. There was an abundance of fig trees on most of these farms. There wasn't a lot peaches, and what they had were pressed peaches, which had a very large seed or kernel in them. There were a lot of plum trees along with those fig trees, and they did better than any of those apples. There were some wild cherries. Along in July you might see a few grapes, not many. When it comes to blueberries, they're very good here.

July was that month of really harvesting, and it was a special challenge to have a ripe watermelon by the Fourth of July. That was sort of a bragging right. Later on in July, watermelon was a refreshment. You'd pick one and put it in the shade, and when you were working in the fields when it got hot about two to three o'clock in the afternoon, oh my, that was refreshment more so than any kind of soda.

In July, you also want to harvest your seeds from the old collard plants.

AUGUST

Some of the running bean varieties would continue to bear on into August, more than the bush varieties we have today. Over middle to late August, the bush varieties are just gone. In the older times, these would bear right into the fall. Of course, you're still eating from the smokehouse, and it could be getting a little rancid in August from the high heat, but that's what they had. They were still doing some fishing when it was possible, but those fresh vegetables, they have really gorged themselves on them now. They've gotten them canned, and maybe now they're starting to use some of those canned vegetables.

It's starting to rain a lot from late July to August, on the average. Everything's just steamy and wet and hot when you're outside. Even in the house cooking, everything's just hot before air conditioning. But one thing that stands out in my mind—peanuts. If you could get them planted in April, it's time for fresh peanuts in August. They will be boiled, and of course they will be green peanuts right off the plant. That earthy smell, taking them right off the plant, washing off the soil and boiling right then, and the smell was just like the smell of fresh, clean earth. If you've ever experienced that, you know what I'm talking about.

You're getting pears in late August and scuppernong and muscadine grapes. Most homes had a grape vine, and in August, you're getting an abundance. Anybody who was going to make wine, when those grapes came off, of course they were eating them fresh, but over the last of August and into September, they were going to start and dry up, so they would have picked them off then to make wine if they were going to make wine because they were at their sweetest stage before they started to fall off. That's when they're most enhanced with sugar, which increases the amount of alcohol.

In August, most of your pears and most of your apples would be in August and September, and there were even fall apples in October. But it's hard to grow a lot of fruit here in the Lowcountry. Most fruit needs pretty cold weather to cause the tree to be dormant enough to set fruit and blossom. Plus there's a lot of disease that affects fruit. There's very few varieties that do well here in tree fruit.

In August, you also want to transplant collard plants. In late August [and] September, you're also going to want to start planting your cole vegetables again. Your cabbage, your mustard greens, your turnip greens and all that for the fall season.

Field peas or cowpeas tolerate heat well, so they may have some in late August or September, and they were eating them green—green peas that hadn't dried. But those were going to dry down after frost. That's when they were going to harvest those dried peas and beans in the lima bean family. They were dried on the plant, in the hull to protect them from insects, and they'd thresh them out. Then they'd wash them and cook them.

They would be drying a lot of things in August, like butterbeans, fruit, tomatoes, okra, green beans, if they chose to preserve them that way. Just put them out in the sun on the warm hot days, and let the sun do the drying. If it started to rain, of course, you'd take them inside, put them in the attic if you had room.

Pea hulls were fed to the livestock, but not the butterbean hulls. On the lima bean, hulls are a little sharp point that will actually penetrate your finger, and they were afraid it would prick the intestines of the animals and irritate it.

September

If you haven't got your cole vegetables in, it's time to get them planted. You're still eating out of the smokehouse, and it's beginning to get slim. You're looking forward to some fresh pork, and you can't wait until it's cold enough to do that.

September is your fruit month for apples, pears, peaches if you could grow them. They're going to begin to get pretty sweet, like the scuppernongs.

OCTOBER

In October, you're beginning to hunt small game again—squirrel, 'possum, raccoon, rabbit. The new offspring of those animals have gotten big enough to survive on their own, and now you can go hunting and harvest them again. The insects are starting to go away that would be on the animals.

Your fish are going to sort of retroactively do what they did in the spring. As they rose in shallow waters and spawned, now they're going to start to go down again. And before it gets real cold, they're going to be in cool, deep holes, but it's still warm enough in the fall where they'll take bait.

If you live close enough to the ocean, of course you've got the run of the saltwater fish that are going to migrate south from the north. September is a very important fishing time at the beach. Most of the time, mullets would run first, then with your spots. There would be people down there fishing and netting right on into the first of November. September and October, a lot of food would have been based around the saltwater fish, whatever they were able to catch at the beach if they were close enough and had means to get there and spend the time.

The sugar cane harvest started late October if they had a patch of cane. The sweet potato harvest is in October. You've got those fresh sweet potatoes even in November. You're harvesting your cole vegetables in October and November before the frost really sets them back.

NOVEMBER

In November, you were looking forward to Thanksgiving. My father's side of the family around Thanksgiving would always butcher a pig. They were out of meat, and the only fresh meat they would have had was wild game and poultry. The smokehouse was about cleaned out. They could butcher a shoat, which is maybe 100–125 pounds at that time, and consume that whole animal before it had time to spoil. At this time, they had an overabundant appetite for fresh pork because they ate salt pork all summer long and had no fresh meat except for fish or poultry.

Coming up to Thanksgiving, that special time, they enjoyed going hunting and having fresh pork butchered.

Sometimes there wasn't enough room—or chairs—inside the house for extended family gatherings, but people made do outdoors with sawhorse tables and plank benches. *Photo circa 1930–50 by William Van Auken Greene. William Van Auken Greene Collection, Horry County Museum, Conway, South Carolina.*

Pecans were harvested in September, October. A lot of black walnut trees were around, and they were harvested. Hickory nuts, too, but most hickory trees around here are wild, and there wasn't much meat in that nut and [it] was very hard to get shelled out. You don't see very many black walnuts still around, but there are a lot of pecan trees. The old black walnut would be very good in cakes.

It was very common to have buckets of pecans sitting around in the kitchen. Kids would have pecans in their pockets. You'd quit work and people would be standing around talking, and they'd pull pecans out of their pocket. You can crack pecans in your hand by putting two nuts together and force them together with pressure. They were a snack; they were everywhere.

Nuts would be on the ground everywhere in November, and the hunting of small animals continued. You'd try to fish a little bit in deep water, use the right bait and all that.

DECEMBER

Then getting into December, you're coming off that fresh pork. Your cole vegetables, if they have survived, you're going to try to preserve them and get that done because they're not going to tolerate freezing two or three nights in a row.

Christmas dinner is based around a lot of that fresh meat that's around, and they'd maybe even butcher another hog. One of my dad's favorites was to take fresh ham and boil it in water with no salt. They'd submerge it in boiling water and boil it until it cooked it all the way through. And take it out, it's whole, and slice it with a knife and sprinkle it with raw salt. And oh my. He just loved that at Christmastime.

If they could raise turkeys, they could have had turkeys for Christmas dinner, but not every farm had turkeys. But every farm did have chickens.

Mr. Alfred G. Trenholm (third from left) entertains telephone switchboard employees, who "manned" the switchboard around the clock in his home on Christmas in 1914. The lady fifth from the left is Miss Sadie Prince; the others are unknown. *Morgan-Trenholm Collection, Georgetown County Library, Georgetown, South Carolina.*

Field Peas

Leona Capps, Conway

Put ¼ cup bacon drippings in a large saucepan and add 1 quart of shelled field peas, with a few cut green snap peas. Steam the peas for a little while without adding any water. In a teakettle or separate pan, boil enough water to cover the peas. Pour the boiling water over the peas and cook for 30–45 minutes.

Chapter 13

POSTWAR BOOM

During World War II, Alzata Lee of Murrells Inlet worked at Garden City Grill, which was located off U.S. 17 Business in Garden City, where there is currently a Walgreen's drugstore. "You could stand there and look straight down to Garden City and see the island," she said. "In '42, '43, '44, I worked there. You had to put a board over a ditch to get there—there was no road to it. It was just a little island over there by itself."

After World War II, a healthy tourist economy turned into a thriving seasonal boomtown. More visitors came, which meant more restaurants were needed to feed them. Visitors were introduced to southern specialties, but also new residents from "away" opened restaurants that introduced locals to new foods.

In September 1946, Tony and Angie Thompson and their infant son, Dino, rolled into Myrtle Beach in a two-tone LaSalle. The first place they stopped, as Dino Thompson recalled in his book *Greek Boy Growing Up Southern*, was the Kozy Korner Café at 819 Main Street, which in earlier years was the Kozy Korner Tavern.

The Kozy Korner Café, which had a two-hundred-item menu offering everything from lobster Thermidor to chow mein, was downtown in the old part of Myrtle Beach, near where First Avenue South turns into First Avenue North, across Kings Highway from the former Myrtle Beach Pavilion amusement park site. An hour after first laying eyes on the triangular-shaped building, Dino said that his dad purchased the restaurant.

"In those days there was the Broadway Restaurant, Seven Seas, the Myrtle Beach Grill and the Kozy Korner," Dino said in a 2002 interview.

Tony and Angie Thompson owned the Kozy Korner in downtown Myrtle Beach from 1946 to 1959. Their son, Dino Thompson, is still a Myrtle Beach restaurant owner. *Author's collection.*

Also in 1946, near the current Bowery building on Ninth Avenue North was an oceanfront tavern appropriately named Ocean Front Tavern.

The Thompsons owned the Kozy Korner until 1959. Dino was the manager during the final three years, while his parents ran another Myrtle Beach restaurant called Black Angus Steak House. After his parents gave up the lease, Dino said, it became a White Castle knockoff called Kings Kastle. "Then it became the first pizza joint off the boulevard—Pizza Villa." In recent years, that site has been a succession of restaurants, from Mexican and Caribbean to its current form (as of spring 2013), an Ohio-style pizza restaurant called Gem City Pizza.

South of Myrtle Beach in Murrells Inlet, more restaurants were opening. In 1947, Mack M. and Teeny Vereen Oliver stopped taking boarders at the waterfront fishing lodge Mack's parents opened in 1910, and Oliver's Lodge became a hugely successful restaurant.

"We always had a waiting line," the late Maxine Oliver Hawkins (1930–2006) said in a 2002 interview. She was Mack and Teeny's daughter and said that there was always a line of customers going out the front door, wrapping around the old live oak trees and going down the dirt road that is now U.S. 17 Business.

The Olivers specialized in $1.25 seafood platters with shrimp, fish, scallops, oysters and deviled crab. One cook's sole job was to drop batter into hot grease to keep up with demand for the popular corndodgers. Desserts were pies made with whatever fruit was in season.

In those days, many young African Americans worked as "creek boys" for the restaurants and for families, gathering crabs, clams and oysters and selling them. Roosevelt "Rooster" Pickett was one of those creek boys who knocked on the back door of Oliver's Lodge in the 1950s and asked Teeny Oliver if she'd like to buy his seafood. She did, and it was the beginning of a good relationship—Rooster lived upstairs at the historic restaurant for most of his life while performing a number of culinary jobs. Maxine sold Oliver's Lodge in 1992, and new owners remodeled it. However, it closed in 2009, and as of May 2013, it is not open for business.

Also in 1947, Capt. Juel's Hurricane Restaurant opened at the Little River waterfront. It was operated by Mary Juel, whose husband was a fishing boat captain named Frank Juel. Beside the restaurant was the couple's fish market, and of course, the restaurant specialized in fresh, local seafood. In the mid-1970s, Joseph and Deanna Robertson bought Capt. Juel's, and according to the restaurant's website, they still operate it as of 2013.

In 1948, Eford and Pearl Lee, who had experience managing Murrells Inlet restaurants called Lokey's and Charlie White's, bought a small former filling station and bar in Murrells Inlet at a tax sale for $800. They called it Lee's Inlet Kitchen and served three meals a day. At first, the seafood restaurant had forty seats in two tiny rooms, and restrooms were outside.

Alzata Lee was Eford's twenty-year-old sister, and she was the restaurant's first waitress. Alzata and the other servers had custom-made uniforms in colors such as pink, blue and purple, and they'd arrange to wear the same colors each day. Back then, liquor was not served in Grand Strand restaurants, and customers brought their own, discreetly sleeved in brown bags. Alzata remembered that some of the more upstanding citizens who didn't want to be seen drinking in public left their bottles in their cars and frequently excused themselves to the parking lot for refreshment.

"Pearl and me run the front, and Eford and a cook, they run the back," Alzata said. "We didn't have hardly any business—we had the Garden City Grill and Oliver's Lodge to compete with."

A 1948 menu from Lee's Inlet Kitchen lists "breakfast" for seventy-five cents, aspirin for ten cents, cigarettes for twenty cents a pack and a newspaper for a nickel. A hamburger was a quarter, shrimp cocktail cost thirty-five cents and lobster tails were two dollars.

Traditional seafood meals included shrimp creole, shad roe, soft-shell crabs (crabs harvested when they've shed their hard outer shell and can be fried and eaten whole) and oyster stew, but the biggest seller was the seafood platter, which sold for $1.50 and was heaped with fried shrimp, oysters, scallops, deviled crab and fish. That fried seafood was cooked in a light and crispy batter known as Lowcountry style, which features bigger pieces of seafood than another fried style popular in later years at Myrtle Beach–area buffet restaurants called Calabash style.

Competition was fierce among the handful of Murrells Inlet restaurants trying to lure customers in for seafood platters. "When they first opened here," Kelly Lee Dorman said, "the Seafood Platter was $1.50. When they went up a quarter to $1.75, everybody went to Lokey's. Then he raised his prices too, and they came back."

In 2013, Lee's Inlet Kitchen entered its sixty-fifth year of business. Billy Lee, who was Eford and Pearl Lee's son at Lee's Inlet Kitchen, took over management of the restaurant as his parents eased into retirement. Pearl passed away in 1975, and Eford died in 1983. Billy was going to sell it after his father died, but his daughter and son-in-law, Kelly and Dexter Dorman, bought it, and the family's third generation started operating the restaurant. Billy Lee passed away in 1992, but Alzata Lee, who will turn eighty-five on December 6, 2013, still works at the restaurant as a hostess.

Lee's Inlet Kitchen has expanded five times through the years, from ten tables that accommodated forty diners to its current capacity of three hundred, and it is still serving seafood platters, shrimp salad, clam chowder and she-crab soup. The Dormans ushered the restaurant into modern technology with computerized point-of-sale systems, pagers for the servers and social media, but the food preparation is still old-school.

"Our seafood is the best we can buy," Kelly Lee Dorman said. "Our flounder and oysters are from North Carolina, our shrimp is from McClellanville and Georgetown and we still peel our own fantail shrimp. We do 150 pounds per night in the summertime—the salad girls, busboys, some of the kitchen help—they're all back there peeling shrimp. They'll stand back there and peel and peel and peel and peel." Other seafood the restaurant uses comes right from Murrells Inlet, such as crab and fresh fish from a local market called Seven Seas Seafood, which has its own fishing boats.

While more diners are opting for broiled or grilled seafood these days, Dorman said that about 75 percent of their customers still opt for fried. Their recipes, largely unchanged for sixty-five years, have resulted in third- and fourth-generation descendants returning to Lee's Inlet Kitchen year after year.

As Lee Brockington noted in *Pawleys Island: A Century of History and Photographs*, during the 1940s, Pawleys Island had an ice cream shop, the Rusty-Ann Restaurant, a bar and restaurant serving seafood called The Towers and "the flat-roofed Wagon Wheel restaurant [which] served hamburgers, seafood and beer."

A young man named Hubert Hoskins and his wife, Leona Eason Hoskins, moved away from the Grand Strand and spent a few years running a tavern in Baltimore. Leona became homesick, and in 1948, they moved back to Ocean Drive Beach (which is what North Myrtle Beach was called at the time) and opened Hoskins Restaurant, the "Home of Finer Food" that was "Located on Main Street Two Blocks from the World's Widest Strand."

At first, Hoskins was located across Main Street from its current location in an inn, but it wasn't long before the location at 405 Main Street was built and ready for customers. Hoskins started with one room and about sixty seats, and the first menu listed a deluxe jumbo hamburger with fries for $0.65 and oyster or crab cocktail for $0.50, while a shrimp cocktail went for $0.60. A beef tenderloin steak was $2.50, and one half golden fried chicken with fries, slaw, corndodgers and coffee or tea was $1.50. The combination seafood platter that was selling for $1.50 down in Murrells Inlet cost $1.75 at Hoskins. The restaurant was also known for Leona's homemade cream pies, such as lemon, pineapple, coconut and chocolate.

In 1956, Hubert passed away, and then Hubert and Leona's daughter, Joan Hoskins Floyd, and son-in-law, J. Bryan Floyd, bought the restaurant. Floyd was the mayor of North Myrtle Beach from 1974 to 1980, and he developed Bay Tree Golf Plantation and helped build the Possum Trot and Robber's Roost golf courses. While the Floyds owned Hoskins, two of Bryan Floyd's brothers operated it part of the time, and at the end of their ownership, their son, Keith Floyd, and his wife ran it.

"After my Dad and Mom bought it from my grandmother, she stayed here and worked and helped out," said current Hoskins owner Tina Floyd Yates, who bought the restaurant in 1989 with her husband, Lenton Yates.

Tina worked at the restaurant starting at age thirteen and continued as seasonal help during her spring and summer breaks from college. Leona Hoskins lived to be almost ninety years old, and she was still golfing well into her eighties and would stop by Hoskins Restaurant on her way home for a fish sandwich and a beer. Bryan Floyd passed away in 2004, and Joan Hoskins Floyd died in 2008.

Over the years, the restaurant expanded from the "front room" to include the "side room" and the "back room," where many area clubs held meetings and private parties were thrown. When the Yateses bought it, they downsized a little and returned the restaurant to two rooms—front and side.

Today, Hoskins Restaurant still serves many of the same recipes that Leona Hoskins cooked, including her cream pies, meatloaf, fried chicken, fried seafood and salmon patties. On peak summer days, the staff peels seventy-five pounds of shrimp, and there's a line of customers down the block waiting for turnip greens, whole fried spot in season, whole fried flounder, chicken and pastry, chicken bog, chopped barbecue, field peas, steamed cabbage, corn with okra and tomatoes, rice and gravy and squash casserole.

Down at the other end of the Grand Strand in Georgetown, Jessie Williams Holtzscheiter had a boardinghouse where anyone could come have lunch for one dollar. Many did, including workers at nearby International Paper Company. Holtzscheiter's niece, Becky Ward Curtis, and nephew, Don Camlin, said that she had a sign on the wall that read, "Take all you want, but eat everything you take."

"It was all country cooking like country-style steak, four or five different meats, six or seven vegetables, lima beans with ham hocks, rice, pork, chicken, roast," Curtis said.

Back in Murrells Inlet, Lokey's Restaurant had been open since the early 1940s, but the owner became disgusted after an employee let wartime-rationed grease for the fryers spill all over the floor. He closed the doors, and it was empty for a while before Jim and Lucy Bailey bought it in 1955 and named it the Wayside.

A deluxe shore dinner with clam chowder, shrimp cocktail, fish, scallops, oysters, shrimp, deviled crab, lobster tail, coleslaw, French fries, ice cream and tea or coffee was $3.00. A pair of Danish or African lobster tails also went for $3.00, and the seafood platter cost $1.50. They served swordfish steak, one-half fried chicken, T-bone steak, burgers, ham and egg sandwiches and their famous shrimp salad. For dessert, there was pie or ice cream for $0.20.

The Baileys' brother, Sam Vereen, worked at the Wayside for a while and then left to help open the Chanty House restaurant (a fellow there actually sang sea chanties) in Murrells Inlet and Rice Planters Restaurant in Myrtle Beach. In 1963, at age twenty-four, Sam Vereen bought the Wayside and operated it for twenty years.

"I picked my help up about ten o'clock in the morning," he said. "None of the help had cars except for the waitresses. I mean you're talking about before integration. I had an old bus I picked everybody up in to come to work. They got off when we closed, which was anywhere from ten o'clock to twelve o'clock at night. They were long days." He continued,

WAYSIDE

MENU

Satisfied guests are our best guarantee of good business. We are anxious to hear any suggestions you may wish to make. In this way we can correct them for your fellow tourist.

LUCY and JIM BAILEY, Props.

U. S. HIGHWAY 17 — MURRELLS INLET, S. C.

Lucy and Jim Bailey sold the Wayside Restaurant in Murrells Inlet to Sam Vereen in 1963. *Sam and Russell Vereen.*

"So everybody came in at the same time. We had four, five head back there peeling shrimp for hours. They peeled 100 to 150 pounds of shrimp a night, peeled and butterflied."

Sarah Gary, born in 1939, worked for Sam Vereen at the Wayside restaurant and currently does prep work and some cooking for Sam's son, Russell Vereen, at Vereen's Seafood Grill, which was founded in 1993 across the street from the Wayside site. Gary's mother, Rebecca "Blossom" Carr, also worked for Sam Vereen.

Back in the day at the Wayside, Sarah Gary peeled up to two hundred pounds of shrimp per day. "Everyone called me the shrimp peeling whiz," she said. "I did the peeling, and others did the slicing and deveining."

The restaurant business boomed in Murrells Inlet, as it did in other parts of the Grand Strand during the 1960s, '70s and '80s. In 1968, descendants of Myrtle Beach's Captain Marshall Holmes Nance founded Nance's Creekfront Restaurant in Murrells Inlet. Many Myrtle Beach visitors either went to Murrells Inlet or Calabash, North Carolina, for their seafood dinners.

"It was like a fair down here every afternoon," Russell Vereen said. "People would come down to Murrells Inlet to watch head boats back up and offload fish. The guys were out there bottom fishing for black sea bass, snapper, vermillion. And when the boats back up, people thronged down here like the circus was in town to watch these boats. You had local boys making a hustle cutting fish on the docks, cleaning them for the guys, seafood markets were cleaning fish for people."

With increasing numbers of tourists, culture clashes occasionally happened. "Right after I opened the Wayside in 1963," Sam Vereen said, "I was walking by this table. We were starting to get a few people out of Litchfield with summer homes who were fairly classy. I was walking through the dining room, and this lady called over to one of the waitresses, and she said, 'Is everything on this menu à la carte?' and [the waitress] said, 'No ma'am, we ain't got nary a thing on a cart.'"

Sam Vereen sold the Wayside in 1983, and since then, it has been several different restaurants. Currently it is called the Hot Fish Club.

In those early days, the restaurant business was even more seasonal than it is today. "We stayed open [at the Kozy Korner] all year," Dino Thompson said, "but [after Labor Day] business didn't slow down—it came to a stop. You could rent the highway out…Everybody engaged in the tourist business. Everybody had to borrow money in the off-season to pay the bills."

Of course, not everyone worked in the restaurant or service industries. Many still farmed and hunted. There were more officeworkers and government jobs, and others worked in the food industry peripherally. People still living on farms had income selling eggs, chickens, pork and produce to restaurants and boardinghouses, while fishermen in Georgetown, Murrells Inlet and Little River kept businesses supplied with seafood.

WAYSIDE RESTAURANT SHRIMP SALAD

Russell Vereen, Murrells Inlet

1 salad bowl full of boiled shrimp, chopped
2 hardboiled eggs, chopped
1 handful sweet salad pickle cubes
1 handful celery, finely chopped
2 heaping tablespoons cottage cheese
1 heaping tablespoon mayonnaise or salad dressing
salt and pepper, to taste

Mix all ingredients well and garnish with onion, bell pepper, tomato and lemon wedges, a few whole boiled shrimp and paprika.

Chapter 14

CONDOS AND CURRENT TIMES

Starting in the latter half of the 1950s, the Myrtle Beach and surrounding Grand Strand areas saw phenomenal growth in hotel construction, and accordingly, the number of new restaurants surged.

"After Hurricane Hazel (in 1954), there was a rash of building," Dino Thompson said. "In the 1960s, [the restaurant industry] burst open. In the 1970s, [developers] discovered the word condominiums. In the 1980s, there was just more of everything. And in the '90s, national chains changed everything."

"Myrtle Beach, from [the 1950s], took off," Dino Drosas said. His family opened Mammy's Kitchen in 1957. "In the 1950s, there were about ten restaurants on the boulevard; in town, there were about six or seven. There was a Howard Johnson's nearby—them and Mammy's Kitchen were the two big restaurants. We had a very, very busy restaurant…Mammy's had lines around the corner almost all day long."

In the 1950s, Jean Chestnut Lee Cribb was living on her family's five-hundred-acre tobacco farm about eight miles north of downtown Myrtle Beach. She didn't even visit a restaurant until she was about twelve years old, when she went with her father to a Conway tobacco warehouse. "We stopped and got a hamburger at Bob's Grill outside Conway on the old highway," she said in 2002. "I thought that was so neat, that you could buy food someone else fixed."

Jack Bourne of Myrtle Beach—who has an immense collection of vintage local restaurant menus, photos, postcards and matchbook covers—said that other restaurants of that period included 20th Century Kitchen in Myrtle Beach, which sold pancakes, waffles and seafood; the Good Food 17 Restaurant; Broadway Restaurant; Seven Seas; the Myrtle Beach Grill; and the Pink House, which was a fine dining restaurant at Forty-third Avenue North and Kings Highway serving dishes such as she-crab soup and baked Alaska and had a buffet with thirty items. The Periscope was a rambling "roadside establishment offering rooms and meals at 2301 North Ocean Boulevard."

Bourne said that his aunt, who is in her eighties as of 2013, remembers dining at Hare's Grill, which was at the corner of Broadway Street and U.S. 501 (501 was called the Conway Highway at the time). His matchbook from Hare's Grill lists its phone number as "5147." Hare's Grill became the Silver Hook Restaurant. "The Silver Hook had the best barbecue plate in town," Bourne said. "They served seafood, steaks—it was a very popular blue plate lunch spot as well. They served blacks out of a walk-up window near the back door, I heard."

Clay Nance noted:

> *I remember the Silver Hook. I remember it in the mid- to late '70s. It was the very first place I ever saw a condom machine in the men's room. It was a very truck stop, meat-and-three, Mel's Diner "kiss my grits" sort of a place. Sherril's Pharmacy was in the Chapin Company building. It had a lunch counter, and I liked their milkshakes. They had an odd square ice cream scooper that they would push down into the ice cream and pull back up. It had a pistol grip, and it would pull up a square hunk of ice cream… My favorite restaurant growing up was Rosa Linda's. In my high school era, we were some Rosa Linda's lovin' people.*

There were three Rosa Linda's Tex Mex restaurants owned by the Favata family, and the last original one closed in 2003.

"Drugstores were always a good place to eat," Bourne said. "We had Delta, Colonial Drugs with a lunch counter and fountain. Walgreens had a luncheonette and served Coble ice cream. Wilma's Cafeteria was next door to Mammy's on the left side; a parking garage is there now. Howard Johnson's…was also a local favorite…It's amazing what you could get for a couple bucks."

In the 1960s, a few Myrtle Beach restaurants included Thomas Cafeteria (which sold genuine Kentucky Fried Chicken); Bell's 19-cent Hamburgers; Hayley's Drive-in; the Henry Grady Restaurant; Seaside Cafeteria a little south of the Pavilion; Lloyd's of Myrtle Beach; and Sloppy Joe's by the Pavilion, the place that dozed but never closed.

In the early 1960s, there was the Hawaiian Village, a Polynesian-inspired motel and dinner theater that was the site of many local proms. It burned down in 1974.

There were Holland House Restaurant at 101 South Kings Highway; Anne's Restaurant at 409 South Kings Highway (where Ho Wah is in 2013); Wink's Drive-In near Fourteenth Avenue South; Long Bay Restaurant and Pancake House, which also sold seafood and had a dance floor for shag dancing; and Jimmies Hamburgers at Eighth Avenue North on Kings Highway.

Up in Atlantic Beach, which is a small community of a few blocks within North Myrtle Beach, the Hotel Gordon served food, and the Hotel Marshall claimed to have the area's "finest inn food and barber shop." Atlantic Beach—also called the Black Pearl—was the only beach in the area before civil rights and integration where African Americans were welcome.

In the mid-1960s, Wade O. "Buster" Camlin had a restaurant on the south causeway in Pawleys Island called the Tee-Pee Drive-In. "It looked like an old tipi building," said Camlin's daughter, Becky Ward Curtis. "He had barbecue and hamburgers." About that time, Buster Camlin's sons, Don and Wade Camlin, bought the fifteen acres along U.S. 17 in Pawleys Island between the two causeways. On one and a half acres of the property, the Camlin brothers built a new restaurant for their parents called Camlin's Restaurant.

"In 1968, we handed Momma the key and said, 'It's yours,'" Don Camlin said. "It was a nice little restaurant. The nearest restaurants in those days was Billy Clair, [who] had the Plantation House on the north causeway, and then the next closest was Oliver's Lodge, Lee's Inlet Kitchen and the Wayside."

"Daddy had to do everything himself," Curtis said. "He wouldn't delegate. When the cooks came, the fish were already scaled and clean—he started at 7:00 a.m. with an electric scaler. They were both the workingest people."

Curtis and Camlin said that that in addition to his pit-cooked barbecue, their father was known for his fish stew. He started giving the tomato-based spicy stew as complimentary samples, and once diners were hooked, it became the top-selling menu item. Camlin's also served steamed local oysters, deviled crab, shrimp salad and shrimp creole. Dell Camlin baked pies and cakes at home to take to the restaurant, such as pound cake, red velvet cake, German chocolate cake, pecan pie, coconut pie and lemon pie. "She also made this lemon cake where when it's hot you drip the juice from the lemon in it," Curtis said. "She'd stick holes in it so the stuff would dribble down in it."

The Long Bay Restaurant and Pancake House in Myrtle Beach served breakfast and "fresh local seafood" and had a dance floor for shaggers. *Author's collection.*

Jean Cribb grew up to marry Billy Lee of Lee's Inlet Kitchen and worked there. After they divorced, she married Ed Cribb, who had been working at Oliver's Lodge since 1960 and lived in the restaurant's upstairs for eight years. In 1971, Jean and Ed Cribb built a restaurant called Chesapeake House on her family's farmland. "When they built the Chesapeake House, everybody told them they were crazy," said Kelly Lee Dorman, Jean and Billy's daughter. "It was the middle of nowhere. I learned to ride bikes on the hill of Lake Arrowhead Road…[where] there used to be an old country store."

Chesapeake House thrived, and it was the first restaurant to open in an area now dense with dozens of restaurants that became known as Myrtle Beach's "Restaurant Row." The Cribbs divorced, but Jean stayed at Chesapeake House to run it until she retired and her sons took it over. Ed Cribb went on to manage and own several more Myrtle Beach–area restaurants.

After his parents sold the Kozy Korner in 1959, Dino Thompson had two successful pancake houses. In 1976, he and Dino Drosas teamed up to open Cagney's Old Place on Myrtle Beach's Restaurant Row, which they furnished with items salvaged from the Ocean Forest Hotel before it was demolished in 1974. Cagney's was known for its dancing room, where shag dancers congregated; its slow-roasted prime rib; and its classically prepared seafood.

Ten years later, Thompson and Drosas teamed up again to open Flamingo Grill at 7050 North Kings Highway in Myrtle Beach. The glamorous Art Deco–style restaurant serves steaks, seafood, chicken and a few Italian dishes and sandwiches.

Cagney's closed in 2012 after thirty-six years in business, but as of spring 2013, Flamingo Grill is still operating.

Through the 1970s, '80s and '90s, the local restaurant industry kept growing, and Myrtle Beach became known for huge buffet restaurants serving Calabash-style fried seafood, which has a light and crispy coating and originated

Camlin's Restaurant in Pawleys Island was known for Buster Camlin's pit-cooked barbecue and fresh seafood. *Becky Ward Curtis.*

in restaurants at nearby Calabash, North Carolina. Steak restaurants catering to golfers opened, and while fast-food restaurants boomed, the local dining scene also began to see more fine dining options.

One such fine dining restaurant, The Library on Kings Highway, has been open since 1974. Breaking away from the fried shrimp and hot dog masses, The Library required that men wear coats and ties, its waiters wore tuxedoes and many dishes such as Caesar salad, sweetbreads, steak Diane and cherries jubilee were prepared tableside. The only aspects that have changed in recent years are a new owner, an updated lounge area and a relaxation of the diners' dress code—male guests are no longer required to wear jackets and ties.

During the last thirty years of the twentieth century, more ethnic and chain restaurants opened in the Myrtle Beach area, like the Boulevard Spaghetti and Pizza Palace, D'Antoni's and the Italian Schooner. Cain's

Restaurant was at Thirteenth Avenue South before it changed to Goody's Flapjacks in the 1980s and then became an International House of Pancakes in the '90s. Villa Romana opened in 1985 on Kings Highway, and an accordion player there still entertains diners.

Russell Vereen of Murrells Inlet remembered getting memorable soul food at Miss Francis' Kitchen on Dunbar Street, which her son and daughter-in-law, Prince and Queenie Bowens, eventually took over. "Miss Francis' Kitchen on the Hill," he called it. "Miss Francis had a place right in the middle of Dunbar Street. It was an old house turned into a restaurant. No two plates matched in the place, ever. They'd come to the table and rattle off 'fried pork chops, fried chicken, stew beef, Salisbury steak,' and you'd pick one and a couple of vegetables, and it would come on a big plate with the cornbread on the top."

In 2012, Queenie Bowens began cooking at Myrtle Beach city councilman Mike Chestnut's restaurant on Sixteenth Avenue North called Big Mike's Soul Food.

Russell Vereen grew up in the Murrells Inlet restaurant community. When his parents, Sam Vereen and Joan Fischler, owned the Wayside, their home was behind the restaurant overlooking the inlet. In 2013, Vereen had his twentieth year as owner of Russell's Seafood Grill and Raw Bar, which is across the street from the former Wayside. He said that he feels privileged to have grown up in a beautiful and tight-knit community before progress made the inlet more urban. He had a boat with a motor since age ten and visited his neighbors by water. Vereen and his friends blocked the creek with shrimp nets when they weren't supposed to and generally lived like "Huckberry Finn with motors."

"And I'm looking at what I grew up with," he said, standing in his restaurant's dining room and gazing over at the site of his childhood home. "Every time I think I don't care for my job any more, I can look right out that window, and I go, 'Shut up, Russell, you can still see it.' It's kind of rare, because the local people have been pushed back. It costs twice as much to live here than it did growing up. It used to be a quiet fishing village."

In 1995, there were 988 full-service restaurants in Horry County, and in 2001, the South Carolina Department of Health and Environmental Control (DHEC) counted 1,405 restaurants. For more than a decade, Myrtle Beach has been ranked as one of the hottest cities in the United States for restaurant growth potential. In 2012, data from Claritas ranked Myrtle Beach at number ten in the United States for growth potential, with

$3,771 restaurant sales per capita and restaurant sales as a percentage of per capita income as 17.68 percent. "The RGI (Restaurant Growth Index) score is calculated on an area's total restaurant sales and sales as a percent of per capita income, compared to the nation as a whole. The national average is 100," according to *Restaurant Business* magazine, and in 2012, Myrtle Beach's RGI was 343.

In a March 28, 2011, article on CNN Money's website, the Myrtle Beach area was ranked as one of the ten fastest-growing cities in the United States. The population of Horry County grew 37 percent from 2000, with 196,629 full-time residents, to 269,291 in 2010, with "about 15 million" annual visitors.

Several restaurants in Horry and Georgetown Counties have been in business twenty years and longer, but they are in the minority. Restaurant buildings change hands frequently—one in the heart of Myrtle Beach has changed ownership, concept and name five times from the end of 2009 through the spring of 2013. "The numbers change daily," said Tom Eshleman, a regional food program supervisor with DHEC in Myrtle Beach.

As of April 1, 2013, Horry County had 1,778 permitted commercial food facilities, and Georgetown County had 331.

BUSTER CAMLIN'S FISH STEW

4 pound white potatoes, peeled, cubed and boiled
4 pounds filleted fish
28 ounces catsup
4 ounces Worcestershire sauce
1½ ounces mustard
¼ pound salt pork
1 onion
1½ teaspoons salt
½ teaspoon red pepper powder
½ teaspoon black pepper

Combine ingredients and heat to desired temperature. Add more pepper for adults.

Chapter 15
PINESAP POTATOES

Jon Leithiser, a Myrtle Beach native, preserves an old cooking method that came about in the eighteenth and nineteenth centuries when the naval stores business boomed in the Grand Strand area. Naval stores are products made from the pitch, or sap, of southern yellow pine trees. The products, such as turpentine, tar and rosin, were important for building and maintaining wooden ships, which were a major transportation mode at a time when rivers and oceans were the world's main highways.

Rivers throughout Horry and Georgetown Counties were lined with turpentine stills, in which the pitch was boiled to remove the turpentine. What was left over was a thick and tarry substance that could be used as a waterproof sealant. When this tar cools, it looks like amber. The solidified rosin can be found all over Grand Strand–area riverbeds. Perhaps it's there because a boat sank, or maybe it was chucked into the river on purpose since the rosin wasn't as valuable as the turpentine.

Jon Leithiser used to do quite a bit of river diving to look for old bottles and other interesting antiquities. He also found rosin, and he brought a few chunks up from the depths and showed them to his brother. "I kept coming across the stuff," Leithiser said in March 2013 as he stirred a cast-iron cauldron full of simmering rosin. "My brother told me there was a restaurant around here that melted it and cooked potatoes in it, and he got the recipe from a guy who worked there."

It was Planters Back Porch Restaurant, which was near the intersection of U.S. 17 and Wachesaw Road in Murrells Inlet. The owners had a wood shack out back containing a cauldron where rosin chunks were melted over a wood fire. Sweet potatoes—with the peels intact—were placed in the slowly boiling pinesap, where they cooked for about thirty minutes, or until the potatoes were floating at the top of the pot.

The potatoes were removed with tongs and slid into brown paper sacks, which were then twisted closed. The pinesap coating on the potatoes cools quickly and forms a hard crust that keeps the potatoes warm for a few hours. When someone is ready to eat one, a knife is used to cut through the paper and crust to expose a creamy and delicious potato. The rosin-coated peel is not eaten.

Turpentine still workers likely knew this method of potato cookery, and that's where and when the practice started in the Grand Strand area. Pine rosin potatoes are not, however, unique to this area. The first edition of *The Joy of Cooking* contained a recipe for them, and Cracker Barrel restaurants served them until 1992.

Area hardware stores used to sell pots full of hardened pinesap for outdoor potato cooking—they were the fried turkey cookers of their day. While pinesap potatoes are deliciously creamy, cooking them is dangerous. The fellow who used to cook them at Planters Back Porch told Leithiser that their potato-cooking shack burned down once in a while. The cast-iron cauldron would be intact, and they'd simply build a new shack.

"You don't want the pinesap to get too hot," Leithiser said. "There's a lot of vapor coming out that can catch fire. It's kind of like cooking gasoline over an open fire." Nevertheless, he still occasionally cooks sweet and white potatoes in pinesap over open fires at friends' parties and special events.

Some sap evaporates, and some clings to the cooked potatoes. As needed, Leithiser adds more sap chunks. When everyone has had their fill of potatoes and it's time to go home, the fire is extinguished and the sap cools. It stays in the pot, hardened, until the next pinesap potato party.

Chapter 16

OYSTER ROASTS

Gathering with friends around a backyard fire and savoring local oysters' sweet brine is one of Grand Strand residents' favorite cool-weather pastimes.

South Carolina oysters are intertidal, which means they live in the pluff mud along creeks and coastal rivers where the ocean tide goes in and out. This type of oyster, as opposed to larger subtidal oysters that are always covered by ocean water, have a relatively thin shell, and several live together in clumped-together masses. These clumps are why local Grand Strand oysters are called cluster oysters.

Four thousand years ago, Native Americans journeyed to coastal areas along the South Carolina coast to harvest oysters and clams. They built fires and roasted them, and they had special hand-sized stone tools to pry shells open so they could savor the oysters' briny sweetness. Through the years, their piles of discarded shells, called middens, grew in height. Sometimes shell middens were left in the shapes of rings—called shell rings—which historian Lee Brockington speculates may have been constructed as palisade walls. A third type of oyster shell pile is called a shell mound, which Brockington said may have been foundations for some type of construction or may have been used as ceremonial sites.

Since Indians first created shell heaps, South Carolinians' love of oyster roasts has not waned. Cooking oysters outdoors over a wood fire is a special part of locals' winter culinary rituals. Cluster oysters are gathered from Murrells Inlet or North Inlet, where there are richly populated oyster beds nourished with recycled oyster shells. Or someone may have visited a local seafood shop to purchase a bushel or two.

If the seafood market didn't wash the oysters, all the sticky pluff mud clinging to them must be rinsed (and sometimes scrubbed) off. A power washer helps a lot with this, and some car washes around the area have special oyster-washing bays.

The backyard oyster pit has to be fired up, which must be done several hours before the roast begins. Most backyard oyster pits are simple structures—perhaps a ring of concrete blocks or a large square of bricks. They can be joined as a permanent structure with mortar, but it isn't necessary. After the wood fire is ignited, it has to be stoked and tended until there's a bed of coals. While the fire-making is going on, it's time to haul out a couple of sawhorses and lay a piece of plywood on top, which is then covered with newspapers. Some folks have wooden picnic tables near their pits.

A few trash bins are needed—one for empty oyster shells and another for trash. Some people have a hole cut in their plywood or picnic table for the oyster shell trashcan to sit under. A five-gallon plastic bucket is filled with water, and a thick beach towel is submerged in it before it's placed near the pit. Hot sauce bottles (Texas Pete should always be one of the choices) are set on the table along with saltine crackers, cocktail sauce, fresh horseradish, lemon wedges and a roll of paper towels. Several rags, old kitchen mitts or work gloves are set around. A few oyster knives are also scattered on the table, but there's no need to worry about having enough for everyone who was invited, as most guests will bring their own.

At the appointed time, people bundled up in jeans, sweatshirts, jackets and hats mosey into the yard. They probably brought a side dish with them such as pimento cheese or sweet potato casserole, or maybe a dessert like pecan pie or pound cake. Bottles of beer and wine are added to coolers full of ice.

When enough folks are gathered to put a hurtin' on the first batch, the host places a piece of metal over the fire. It might be a sheet of salvaged steel or a piece of tin roofing. An old beat-up pot or cast-iron skillet has a stick of butter plunked into it, and it's set on the edge of the metal so the butter can melt.

Finally, it's time to pile oysters on the metal in a single layer. As soon as they're placed, the wet towel is pulled out of the bucket and laid over the oysters. The hot metal creates a great cloud of steam that puffs up the towel like a balloon, sizzling liquid spits and sputters and stomachs start growling.

At this time, the oyster roaster asks his guests if they prefer their oysters wet or dry. Most say medium. After a few minutes, the towel balloon deflates, and the towel is removed and put back in the water bucket. A shovel is used to scoop up the oysters, and they're placed on the newspaper-topped table. The pan of butter is pulled off the fire and put on the table with the other condiments.

Guests whip oyster knives out of their back pockets, grab a rag or glove or oven mitt to protect their oyster-holding hand from hot shells and sharp edges and get busy shucking. Some eat the oysters plain and relish drinking the briny liquid in the shells, called likker (not to be confused with collards' likker). Others open a lot of shells and make a little pile of meaty morsels to enjoy all at once. Sometimes an oyster is placed on a cracker with a dab of hot sauce or cocktail sauce, while a few go for just a squirt of lemon juice and/or a scoop of horseradish. Whichever way they enjoy their oysters, the pile quickly disappears.

With a batch or two of oysters and a beer or three under their belts, someone usually turns on music and remembers that there are side dishes to eat. Outdoor lights are cut on so the party can continue past dark. Everyone carries on until the oysters run out, and then some. It's also common for propane cookers and stockpots to be used for outdoor oyster steaming, which works fine but doesn't have quite the same ambiance.

The day after the roast, the empty oyster shells are taken to a recycling center, and they'll be put back in the water for more oysters to grow on.

Chapter 17

BOILED PEANUTS AND PARCHED PEANUTS

For most anyone who grew up in the Grand Strand area, boiled peanuts are a seasonal salty treat that puts a sparkle in the eyes of those who love them. "When that first batch of the harvest comes to boil," said Wayne Skipper, farm manager at the L.W. Paul Living History Farm outside Conway, "that earthy smell just draws you when they're fresh."

The peanut is another food brought to the Grand Strand by African slaves and slave traders. Food historians agree that the legume originated in South America and that they were taken to Europe by Spanish explorers.

Peanuts were introduced to Africans possibly as early as the 1400s and were quickly accepted because peanuts were similar to

The earthy aroma of fresh green boiled peanuts is irresistible for many Grand Strand–area residents. *Photo by Matt Silfer, Silfer Studios.*

another food familiar to Africans called the Bambara groundnut. However, peanuts were tastier, more nutritious and easier to harvest than Bambara.

The Kongo and Bantu term for peanut is *nguba*, and in the southern sea islands, the Gullah term was *guba* or *gubar*, which eventually became "goober."

In Andrew F. Smith's book *Peanuts: The Illustrious History of the Goober Pea*, he wrote that peanuts were exported from Africa to Jamaica, and from there the nuts made their way to America on slave ships:

> In 1707, the British botanist Hans Sloane collected peanuts in the Caribbean. In the harbor of Port Royal, Jamaica, Sloane found a ship "from Guinea, loaded with Blacks to sell. The Ship was very nasty with so many People on Board. I was assured that the Negroes feed on Pindals or Indian Earth-Nuts, a sort of Pea or Bean producing its Pods under ground. Coming from Guinea they are fed these Nuts or Indian corn boil'd whole twice a day." Sloane acquired part of his information from Henry Barham, who proclaimed in his own book, "Hortus Jamaica," that he first saw peanuts "in a negro's plantation, who affirmed, that they grew in great plenty in their country." Likewise, Patrick Browne in his "Civil and Natural History of Jamaica" reported that peanuts were "frequently imported to Jamaica in the ships from Africa" and were cultivated in very small quantities in Jamaica. So frequently were peanuts brought from Africa that Edward Long, in his 1774 "History of Jamaica," expressed the belief that peanuts were "nourishing, and often given as food to Negroes on voyages from Guiney, where they pass under the name of gubagubs." He noted that the peanuts could "be eaten raw, roasted, or boiled." Yet another report emanated from Fusee Aublet, whose "Histoire des plantes de la Guiane Francoise" recorded that crews fed peanuts to the slaves on their passage from Africa…Slave ships coming to America were provisioned with peanuts, and it was through the slave trade that peanuts were introduced into what is today the United States.

The slaves planted peanut patches, roasted and boiled the nuts, added them to soups and stews and ground them into paste. Those who were plantation cooks introduced them to their masters.

However, peanuts didn't become mainstream right away. Many considered peanuts to be food for poor people or even animal fodder, but slowly whites discovered peanuts' tastiness, although until the 1800s, they were commonly called groundnuts, goobers or pindars. It wasn't until 1794, according to Andrew Smith, that an Englishman named Henry Wansey, who was writing about trying the nuts in the United States, referred to them as "pea-nuts."

In 1847, Sarah Rutledge included in *The Carolina Housewife* a recipe for ground-nut soup: "To half a pint shelled ground-nuts, well beaten up, add two spoonsful of flour, and mix well. Put to them a pint of oysters, and a pint and a half of water. While boiling, throw on a seed-pepper or two, if small."

By the mid-1800s, peanuts were being grown and enjoyed throughout the United States, but it wasn't until after the Civil War that their popularity soared. Confederate soldiers during the Civil War scavenging for food thought that peanuts—which they called "goober peas"—were nutritious and staved off hunger pangs quite well. Even better, they were easily portable.

This is where some conventional and oft-retold historic accounts of Civil War peanut eating become muddled. It's often repeated that Confederate soldiers boiled peanuts in salted water as a way to create a handy preserved camp food, and the salt made the peanuts last longer. That could not be true because raw peanuts in the shell stay fresh much longer than boiled peanuts. In fact, if they aren't consumed, refrigerated or frozen after being cooked, boiled peanuts get slimy in a day or two and quickly go bad. Also, salt was a precious commodity for traveling troops—sometimes there was barely enough available to salt and preserve pork for the soldiers—so it's hard to believe that foot soldiers had access to the cup or two of salt necessary to cook up a pot of boiled peanuts.

There is a song about peanuts called "Goober Peas" that was a favorite of Confederate soldiers. It's often said that the song is about boiled peanuts, but nowhere in the lyrics is any reference made to boiling the nuts. In fact, one line refers to "wearing out your grinders, eating goober peas." Boiled peas won't wear out your "grinders," or teeth. They're extremely soft.

It is likely that peanut patches were raided by troops. If the peanuts weren't yet mature, boiling them would make the tiny nuts—or "pops," as they're called at that immature stage—swell up and become more filling. So perhaps the troops boiled the pops, but it's more likely that they ate crunchy peanuts in the shell or roasted them over a campfire. Or, if their grinders were sensitive, which is quite possible in those days before modern dentistry, then maybe, if they had time, they boiled mature raw peanuts, but probably without salt since it was so scarce.

After the War Between the States, the popularity of peanuts increased. Bessie Pringle wrote about keeping peanuts in the shell in her pocket for snacks and to give out to children. It was common for rural folks to have peanuts in their pockets, Wayne Skipper said, and pull them out to eat during work breaks.

Charles Johnson, who grew up in Georgetown in the late 1960s and early '70s, remembered being a parched peanut vendor when he was a child:

Peanut vendors were common after the Civil War. This 1903 photo depicts "a peanut vender of the sunny south." *Photo by John H. Tarbell. Picture Collection, the New York Public Library, Astor, Lenox and Tilden Foundations.*

We had this guy, Bubba Josh, who lived on St. James Street, right down from Mayer Funeral Home. He made a machine that was so ingenious. You put green peanuts into this barrel on a motor, and it would keep turning and it heated up. Every once in a while he'd get one out and say, "No, they're not ready," and he'd let it go another 30 minutes. He even made little carts. We would go down Front Street in Georgetown and sell bags for a nickel and a dime. The carts had two big wheels on them and a bell on it, and we'd be going down Front Street shouting, "Fresh parched peanuts! Get 'em while it's hot!" Bubba Josh wouldn't let them go unless they were hot. We'd sell them, and then he'd give us a dollar or so. He always guaranteed if you found one burned peanut in the sack, he'd give you ten dollars.

Charles's brother, B.B. Johnson, said that he made his own parched peanuts. "You put them in the oven, in the shell, and take the spatula and turn them every now and then so they don't burn," he said. "When it gets to the point where the shells are lifting up, you know it's time to take them out of the shell."

But while parched peanuts are made with mature nuts, boiled peanuts are best when they're green, which is the second or third week of August. At that point, Wayne Skipper explained, a shell has started to form, but a quarter of the nuts inside are still pops. At this point, the nuts have an extremely fresh flavor, and their small size allows them to expand to a manageable size when boiled. "Once [the peanuts] mature," Skipper said, "they fill out the shell so much, when you boil them they expand so much you can't hardly get them open."

Skipper and Living History Farm volunteer Levon Hucks said that the season's first batch of boiled peanuts was eagerly anticipated and quickly consumed. They said that an iron pot was set over an outdoor fire and filled half or two-thirds full with green peanuts in the shell. Water was added to cover them along with "a cup or two" of salt. After they boiled about an hour, it was time to start tasting the peanuts to see if they were done. "You let them simmer after you started eating them," Hucks said. "If you wanted them really salty, you'd leave them in the water overnight, if you had some left. Then they'd be really salty."

Locals still boil green peanuts in season, and some people will make and eat them at no other stage. Others will boil them at other times of the year using raw unsalted peanuts in the shell.

Boiled peanuts are now a common snack food sold at roadside stands throughout the Grand Strand area, and there is a dense concentration of them along U.S. 501 between Conway and Aynor. Big cauldrons bubble, waiting for passersby to stop before they're dipped out into foam cups, with either a second foam cup or a paper bag for the discarded shells as part of the deal. Convenience stores and some grocery stores also have smaller boiled peanut pots, and occasionally they're found with additional flavoring such as Cajun spices.

On May 1, 2006, former South Carolina governor Mark Sanford signed a bill declaring boiled peanuts as the official state snack. The bill reads, "The General Assembly finds that boiled peanuts are a delicious and popular snack food that are found both in stores and roadside stands across the State, and this delicious snack food is defined as peanuts that are immersed in boiling water for at least one hour while still in the shell. The General Assembly further finds that this truly Southern delicacy is worthy of designation as the official state snack food."

BOILED PEANUTS

Benjamin "B.B." Johnson, Georgetown

Place 2 pounds of green peanuts, in the shell, in a large pot and add enough water to cover them by a couple of inches. Sprinkle salt over the top of the batch—start with about 2 heaping tablespoons—and bring to a boil. When it's boiling, taste the water and see if it's salty enough for you. If not, add more salt and repeat the tasting process. When they're salted as desired, add a pinch of sugar to the water. Boil for at least an hour and then take a few out and taste them to see if they're done. The nuts should be soft, but not mushy, and salty.

Chapter 18

FISH AND GRITS

Two foods that the Grand Strand area has in abundance are grits and fish—both fresh and saltwater. Many local old-timers recall breakfasts, lunches and dinners of fish and grits, and the tradition started with Native Americans, who used stones to grind dried corn and made their own nets to catch fish.

While fish and grits was more common inland, coastal dwellers put many types of seafood on their grits. Alzata Lee of Murrells Inlet said that she didn't realize how well they were eating in the 1930s. "The inlet fed us," Lee said in a 2002 interview. "We ate oysters and shrimp for breakfast, with grits over hot biscuits. We'd get oysters out of the creek and put them in a basket with chicken wire around it, so when the tide came in, they'd keep fresh and wouldn't wash away. At low tide, we'd take rakes and rake crabs out. We were eating good and didn't even know it."

"My great-grandmother, Lorine Sherill, one of her side jobs was when the boats came in, she would head shrimp," Aun Johnson of Georgetown said. "The squids used to come in on the boats, and the fishermen would just throw them away, but the people heading shrimp would take them. I remember my great-grandmother would fry them up and put gravy on it. We'd have squid and grits."

While shrimp and grits can take on many variations, such as with butter and vegetables or with brown gravy, fish and grits almost always is just fried fish on top of or beside grits. Inland, where only freshwater fish were easily available and affordable, fish and grits was and still is a common meal for native Horry and Georgetown County families. It's cooked simply, and it's still prepared in the traditional manner at Freshwater Fish Company, located a little north of Conway on SC 701.

These days, ocean fish are more readily available at inland areas, so diners at Freshwater Fish Company have choices of spot, croaker, perch, mullet, catfish, bass and flounder. Small fish such as spot and croaker are fried whole (except for the head), and two of them are placed atop white grits.

The annual African American Community Coalition Fish Fry held in November at Belin United Methodist Church in Murrells Inlet serves fish and grits, and several other area restaurants still serve it. A few are Capt. Juel's Hurricane Restaurant in Little River, Sea Captain's House Restaurant on Ocean Boulevard in Myrtle Beach, Aunny's Country Kitchen in Georgetown and Litchfield Restaurant in Pawleys Island.

Watch out for bones—small fish fried whole contain a lot of them. "Food like that, it's taught to the children because you have to learn how to eat it," Charles Johnson of Georgetown said. "I never had a fillet until college. You have to learn how to eat it with the bones. And everyone has had the bone stuck in the throat, and then you give them the milk and the bread to work it down. After a while, they cut that apron string and give you the fish, and you have to learn to eat it without the bone going down."

The River Room Restaurant, which has been in business for almost thirty years beside the Georgetown waterfront, is known for its shrimp and grits. If you would rather make fish and grits, simply use the grits recipe here and top it with fried fish.

RIVER ROOM'S SHRIMP AND GRITS

(4 servings)

THE GRITS
3 cups water
salt, to taste
1 cup grits
1 cup milk (or heavy cream)
butter, salt and pepper to taste

To prepare grits, bring water, salt and grits to a boil. Stir frequently. Lower the heat and reduce grits to a simmer. Add the milk. Cover the pot and simmer for 50–60 minutes, stirring frequently. Add more salt, pepper and butter to taste.

The Sauce
2 cups of ham stock (ham base plus water)
roux (butter plus flour)

To prepare sauce, bring the ham stock to a slight boil, then thicken the stock by adding a small amount of roux. You don't need a lot of roux, just enough to thicken the stock a little bit. (Roux is equal parts butter and flour and is used to thicken many sauces.)

Overall Preparation
small amount of butter
20 shrimp, peeled and deveined
20 slices smoked sausage
thinly sliced Cajun Tasso ham, to taste (it's spicy)
chopped scallions
the grits
the sauce

Place a small amount of butter in a pan. Put the shrimp, sausage and Tasso ham in first and sauté until the shrimp are done. (Don't use too much butter or the sauce will be greasy.) Scoop the grits onto four serving plates. (You can do this while cooking the shrimp and sausage.) When the shrimp are done, add the ham sauce to the pan with the shrimp and stir the mixture around to get all the crusty stuff off the bottom of the pan. (This is what is referred to as deglazing the pan.) Spoon the shrimp and sausage over the grits, garnish with chopped scallions and parsley and serve.

Chapter 19
A FEW MORE HERITAGE FOODS

TERRAPINS AND TURTLES

People in the Grand Strand area have been eating terrapins—freshwater turtles, also called cooters—since Native Americans were the only local residents. Some locals still enjoy turtle soup. Five freshwater species are found in the Grand Strand area: chicken, spiny soft shell (common snapping turtle), Florida cooter, river cooter and yellowbelly. Diamondback terrapins are found in brackish waters.

Massive loggerhead sea turtles, which are the South Carolina state reptile, nest all along the coast here, and they and their eggs were eaten until 1978, when a dwindling population earned the reptile a spot on the endangered species list. Loggerheads can weigh more than 250 pounds, and they live about fifty years. Females return to the same beaches where they hatched when it's time to lay their own eggs, and their nests contain up to one hundred soft and pliable eggs a little larger than ping-pong balls. Females don't stay with their buried nests after laying the eggs, so the eggs are easy pickings for predators.

"That was another food we used to have a lot when we were young," Charles Johnson said. "Guys would go to the beaches and get turtle eggs, real soft eggs. They sell them off the back of their truck. You'd pinch a hole in it and suck the egg out. That was in '62, '63, '64, before it was illegal…I remember when we ate turtle soup, it was with loggerheads. We used to do the turtle like the hog—there was no part of it we wouldn't use. We even used the shell for decoration."

"Diamondbacks were commercially harvested in the 1880s and '90s from these local salt marshes," historian Lee Brockington said. "Plantation hotels, restaurants and trains [served turtle]. Also riverboats…there are really good stories about what particular boats were best for river traffic, because they always had good meals."

Alligator

The rivers of Horry and Georgetown Counties teem with alligators. Before bridges and automobiles, traveling from the western parts of the area to the beach involved two or three days' journey by horse and cart and ferries, and those travelers often camped out in their wagons. During warm months, those overnights would be filled with the roars of bull alligators.

Alligators are good eating, and despite their ferociousness, they've been hunted for centuries. B.B. Johnson remembered watching some of his friends hunt them in the Georgetown area. "When guys saw a young alligator, they'd grab him and hold him until he stopped moving around. Then they took a knife to strip it." The meat, Johnson said, would then be grilled or fried. Alligator meat is a white meat, and yes, it does taste a little like chicken.

A few area restaurants serve fried alligator chunks, and Preston's Seafood and Country Buffet in North Myrtle Beach serves alligator sausage.

Neckbone or Backbone Gravy and Rice

"My grandmother used to make her neckbone gravy with hardboiled egg in it," Aun Johnson said. "That was the best gravy." Leona Capps (1918–2010) of Conway loved having friends over for meals, and backbone gravy and rice is a specialty she served at a 1998 luncheon. The dish isn't fancy—it's a recipe she learned growing up on a farm with ten siblings—but it is exceedingly delicious.

LEONA CAPPS'S BACKBONE GRAVY AND RICE

*Cook a pork backbone in water until done (Leona Capps bought a whole pork loin and
had the butcher slice it and wrap the backbone separately). Take the bone out of the
broth and remove the meat; reserve.*
*Add 1 cup of rice for each 2 cups of broth in the pan. Sift in a little red pepper, to taste,
and add the reserved backbone meat. Cover and simmer until rice is cooked.*
*For the gravy, use canned chicken broth or bouillon. Use however much broth as you
need servings. Put the broth in a saucepan and add 2 chopped hardboiled eggs. Mix in 2
tablespoons of cornstarch and a little black and red pepper. To serve, let guests pour the gravy
over a helping of rice.*

CRAB

Blue crabs harvested off the shores of the Grand Strand are scrumptious.
All you need to snag a few out of muddy tidal areas is a raw chicken neck
or leg, a piece of string and a net. Simply tie the chicken to the string and
cast it out in the water. After a few minutes, slowly pull in the string, and
if a crab has latched on, use the net to scoop it up. There are also crab
pots that can be baited with raw meat. The crab goes in to eat and can't
get back out.

B.B. Johnson of Georgetown remembered netting crabs as a boy as
the tide went out. "Cooking crabs is a lot of fun," he said. "Then you
make crab patties with a little onion and saltine crackers. My grandmother
always did it with her hands—she mixed it up and put it into a patty and
then fried it. She served it near rice. You could take twelve crabs and steam
them and make a meal. We had a soda bottle and would use that to crack
the shells."

It takes patience to pick out the sweet and succulent meat after they're
steamed, but they're worth the effort. An annual Blue Crab Festival is held
on a weekend in the middle of May at the Little River waterfront.

ROE

Sturgeon and shad are the two main roe sources in local fishes, and sturgeon was fished almost to extinction for its eggs.

Sturgeon were once plentiful in almost forty rivers spanning the U.S. eastern seaboard from Maine to Florida, and Winyah Bay at Georgetown was an entryway from the sea for the huge fish (averaging six to eight feet in length and weighing three hundred pounds) to travel upriver and spawn.

In a 2009 article published in the *Winyah Bay Heritage Festival Guide*, Dean Cain wrote, "Four hundred years ago, John Smith credited sturgeon with saving the first English settlement in the North America, Jamestown, from starvation. He claimed that there were so many of the animals that one could walk from one side of the James River to the next on their backs."

Their meat was usually smoked, and the roe was prized as fine caviar. In the Georgetown area, several fishermen made caviar out of sturgeon roe, and two of the most famous were Rene Cathou and Albert Springs "Cap'n Boo" Lachicotte. Cain wrote that in 1984, one year before it became illegal to harvest Atlantic sturgeon in South Carolina, "the value of a 250 pound female 'cow' sturgeon including meat and caviar could reach to $1,500 (paid to the fisherman…the value of the processed caviar to the consumer was much higher.)"

"Fifty percent of our diet was seafood, growing up," said Charles Johnson of Georgetown. "My father, Benjamin Johnson, was a commercial fisherman. When he docked, he'd always bring fish, shrimp and crab home, and we always had to clean it. I didn't realize how great of food we were eating at the time. He brought home shrimp, fish like shad, and during that time sturgeon was legal, so he'd bring a lot of sturgeon home."

"When I was much younger, I saw a lot of sturgeon," said Charles Johnson's older brother, Benjamin "B.B." Johnson. "Mr. Gardiner used to catch the sturgeon, and they were so large he took a ladder to take the height off of it. Most sturgeons are so large you can share. You get close to the meat and cut the portion away that's hard [the outer bony plates, which are called scutes]. With the sturgeon roe, I basically fried mine. Most times you cook that with an egg."

But while it is now illegal to harvest sturgeon, shad roe is still available in the spring. Charles Johnson said that he knows people who scramble shad roe with eggs. "You put the roe in the pan and heat it a little bit, drop an egg in it and scramble it," he said.

Louis Osteen is an esteemed chef who has owned or worked at restaurants in Pawleys Island, Charleston and more. Named in 2004 as the Best Chef in the Southeast by the James Beard Foundation, Chef Osteen is one of the few chefs left in the Grand Strand area who prepares shad roe each spring, and it is one of the five southern foods he thinks are "quintessential." The other four are tomatoes, rice, grits and seafood in general.

"The size of the shad roe varies greatly," Chef Osteen wrote in his 1999 cookbook, *Louis Osteen's Charleston Cuisine: Recipes from a Lowcountry Chef*. This is a major factor in "how long it should be cooked. For that reason, cooking shad roe is one of those times when the old cast-iron skillet borders on being a necessity, because its heavy weight affords an even cooking surface. In this recipe, the roe is incredibly rich and delicious, the bacon adds a crunchy texture, and the capers and lemon add just the right touch of piquancy. The only improvement to this spring favorite would be to put a big dollop of creamy grits on the plate as well."

Shad Roe with Bacon, Lemon Butter and Capers

Chef Louis Osteen, Pawleys Island

4 sets medium to large shad roe
3 cups whole milk
Tabasco sauce, to taste (optional)
8 slices bacon, diced into ¼-inch pieces
⅔ cup all-purpose flour
¾ teaspoon salt
½ teaspoon freshly ground black pepper
9 tablespoons unsalted butter (1 tablespoon for sautéing; the rest cut into 12 pieces)
¾ cup fresh lemon juice
1 cup chopped fresh Italian parsley
4 ounces small capers, drained
¼ cup water
salt and freshly ground black pepper, to taste
creamy grits

Cutting carefully, separate the sets of roe. You will see that there is a logical place to do this close to the center. Be sure not to puncture the membrane, as it holds in the eggs. Place the roe in a nonreactive pan and add enough milk to cover. Add a couple dashes of Tabasco to the milk if you like. Cover the pan and refrigerate for 2 hours.

Cook the bacon in a cast-iron skillet over medium heat until very crispy, turning it as it cooks. Remove to a paper towel to drain, leaving the rendered fat in the pan.

Mix the flour, ¾ teaspoon of salt and ½ teaspoon of pepper in a small bowl. When ready to cook the roe, drain carefully and dredge in the seasoned flour, shaking off the excess.

Add the reserved tablespoon of butter to the bacon fat in the skillet and heat over medium heat. When the butter starts to foam and the bubbles begin to subside, add the roe with the blue vein up. Sauté over medium heat, watching carefully. Shad roe has a tendency to cause the fat to pop and sputter as it cooks. The timing for cooking roe is important and delicate: in the center, it should be cooked about medium, not rare, but not dry and crumbly either, and on the outside, it should be slightly crusty. A 5-inch piece needs about 4 minutes on each side. When cooked, remove the roe to a platter lined with paper towels and cover loosely with aluminum foil while finishing the sauce.

Remove the skillet from the heat. Discard the fat but do not wipe or wash the skillet before proceeding. Add the lemon juice, parsley, capers and remaining 8 tablespoons of butter. Place the skillet back on the heat and add the water. Shake the skillet as the butter melts. This should take about 3 minutes, and the sauce should be slightly thickened. Take the skillet off the heat and add the reserved bacon and then salt and pepper to taste. Stir to combine everything.

Place the shad roe on warm plates, spoon a couple tablespoons of sauce over it and serve with the creamy grits.

Barbecue

In Georgetown from the 1930s until he passed away in 1987, Wade O. "Buster" Camlin was known as one of the area's best barbecue cooks. Raised in Williamsburg County as one of fourteen children of tobacco farmers, he learned at a young age the art of pit-cooked barbecue where wood was burned in a pit and then the coals were shoveled about every thirty minutes, all day long, under racks with hogs on them.

Camlin came to Georgetown in 1929 as the shop manager for a Chevrolet dealership. Eventually, he owned Pontiac, Studebaker-Packard and Mercury dealerships in Georgetown, but when he wasn't working, he loved to cook.

In his roles as a Shriner and a Mason, Camlin was the go-to guy for cooking several hogs at once for barbecue fundraisers.

"At one point, Daddy was cooking for 1,200 people at the Shrine Club," said Buster Camlin's daughter, Becky Ward Curtis. "Clinton Altman Jr., who owns a trucking firm in Atlanta, was about nine years old and jumped over a bonfire, and he fell in the fire. He had to have skin grafts from the neck down. Daddy at that time was a Mason before he was president of the Shrine Club for Georgetown and Williamsburg County. He had a fundraiser to pay for Clinton's surgery."

An undated newspaper clipping that Curtis has notes that her father and his friend W.C. Hunter "once cooked barbecue for 3,800 persons during a S.C. Ports Authority affair."

As with many expert whole hog pit barbecue masters, Camlin was particular about what type of wood he used, according to Curtis:

> *The Shrine Club on Black River Road had huge big old pits. Daddy always talked about how important the wood was for cooking hogs for barbecue. He would only use Black Jack oak wood. I can hear him now saying, "You've got to keep that wood turned and moving." Two people would get one on one side of the hog and one on the other and turn it. There was a certain time you had to cook it. First it was skin-up for eight hours, then they'd turn it over, and all the sudden the skin would start blistering, and you took it off. Daddy always put the crackling to the side and had crackling for everyone to eat.*

"He had barbecue pits at the restaurant [Camlin's Restaurant in Pawleys Island]," said Buster's son, Don Camlin. "When he cooked one time at Pawleys Island, he had a pit that would reach from here to the road with cement blocks for steps on the sides, with a metal rod across and hog wire rolled out. He'd leave a space along the sides to put the coals in there. He got Kraft paper from the International Paper Company and put that on top. He'd roll that paper back and use a kitchen mop to mop the sauce on, then put the paper back. He could cook forty pigs at a time."

"I can remember a whole pile of pigs when he was raising money," said Curtis. "Any time they wanted to raise money in Georgetown, South Carolina, for some benefit or to help a family a little, Daddy ended up cooking."

For years, people begged Buster Camlin for his barbecue sauce recipe, but he always said that he couldn't give it out because he never measured anything. But he did give it to his son, Don Camlin.

BUSTER CAMLIN'S BARBECUE SAUCE

3 gallons vinegar
3 big (serving size) spoons black pepper
1 ounce red pepper powder
6 ounces Worcestershire sauce
3 big (serving size) spoons mustard
3 cups sugar
½ cup salt
32 ounces catsup

Blend ingredients and bring to warm. Do not boil!

Chapter 20
HERITAGE RESTAURANTS

With more than two thousand restaurants in the Grand Strand area, you don't have to look far to find those serving heritage foods, and this list will help you find delicious traditional dining. Please keep in mind that restaurants come and go, so it's a good idea to call ahead and verify that it is still open. Most of these listed here have been in business for many years.

The area code for all these restaurants is 843. The foods listed are just a sampling of what each restaurant offers; many of them change their menus seasonally.

AUNNY'S COUNTRY KITCHEN, 926 FRONT STREET, GEORGETOWN (461-4750)
- fried chicken, whole fried spots, collards, cornbread, hog maw, red rice, Ms. Jane Going's bread pudding

BALL & QUE, 1808 HIGHMARKET STREET, GEORGETOWN (546-6404)
- fried chicken, ham pileau, rice and gravy, lima beans, steamed cabbage, fried okra, candied yams, barbecue, fried seafood platters, crab dip, caramel cake, coconut pie

BIG MIKE'S SOUL FOOD, 504 SIXTEENTH AVENUE NORTH, MYRTLE BEACH (712-2048)
- meatloaf, ribs, collards, fried chicken, macaroni and cheese

BISTRO 217, 10707 OCEAN HIGHWAY, PAWLEYS ISLAND (235-8217)
- pimento cheese, herb-encrusted grouper, pear salad, seared scallop salad, she-crab soup, fried okra, crab cake, fried green tomatoes and oysters

BROOKGREEN GARDENS, 1931 BROOKGREEN DRIVE, MURRELLS INLET (235-6000)
- grilled shrimp 'n' grits, she-crab soup, Lowcountry pimento cheese sandwich, signature Carolina peach tea

CHESAPEAKE HOUSE, 9918 NORTH KINGS HIGHWAY, MYRTLE BEACH (449-3231)
- fish stew, she-crab soup, oyster stew, Carolina crab cakes, Lowcountry shrimp creole, Lowcountry shrimp and grits

CHESTNUT HILL, 9922 NORTH KINGS HIGHWAY, MYRTLE BEACH (449-3984)
- shrimp and grits, fried green tomatoes, crab cakes, she-crab soup, fresh flounder fillet

CHIVE BLOSSOM CAFÉ, 85 NORTH CAUSEWAY ROAD, PAWLEYS ISLAND (237-1438)
- Lowcountry shrimp salad, okra pancakes, oyster pie, deconstructed seafood pileau

CRADY'S ECLECTIC CUISINE, 332 MAIN STREET, CONWAY (248-3321)
- flounder po' boy, fried green tomato BLT, southern caramel cake, double crust fruit pie

FRANK'S AND FRANK'S OUTBACK, 10434 OCEAN HIGHWAY, PAWLEYS ISLAND (237-3030)
- pimento cheese, fried okra, crab fritters, pan-fried grouper and sautéed jumbo lump crab cakes with Carolina stone-ground yellow grits and braised South Carolina collards

FRESHWATER FISH COMPANY, 4640 SC 701 NORTH, CONWAY (365-4915)
- fish and grits, catfish stew, fried blue crabs, fried seafood platter, crab cakes, pound cake

HANSER HOUSE RESTAURANT, 14360 OCEAN HIGHWAY, PAWLEYS ISLAND (235-3021)
- crab cakes, creek shrimp, Lowcountry flounder, chicken or shrimp creole, pork chops with onions rings and applesauce

Hoskins Restaurant, 405 Main Street, North Myrtle Beach (249-2014)
- grits, biscuits, greens, corn with okra and tomatoes, whole fried flounder, fried chicken, seafood platters, cream pies

Kudzu Bakery, 120 King Street, Georgetown (546-1847); 221 Willbrook Boulevard, Pawleys Island (235-8560); and 7223 North Kings Highway, Myrtle Beach (213-0605)
- sweet potato pie, peach pie, rum pound cake

Lee's Inlet Kitchen, 4460 U.S. 17 Business, Murrells Inlet (651-2881)
- clam chowder, she-crab soup, fried seafood platters, shrimp salad

Limpin' Jane's, 713 Front Street, Georgetown (485-4953)
- pimento cheese, po' boy, chicken livers, shrimp and grits, fried seafood platter, crab and scallop cake

Litchfield Restaurant, 12223 Ocean Highway, Pawleys Island (237-4414)
- fish and grits, fried chicken, fried flounder, chicken pilau, turnip greens, lima beans, red rice, crab cake

Little Pigs BBQ, 6102 Frontage Road, Myrtle Beach (692-9774)
- chopped pork barbecue

Louis's at Sanford's, 251 Willbrook Boulevard, Pawleys Island (237-5400)
- pulled pork, fried flounder, roasted pork, sorghum baked beans, squash casserole, collards, preserved duck over grits with redeye gravy, she-crab soup, shrimp and oyster gumbo over rice, shrimp salad, brace of quail, fried seafood platter, shrimp and grits, skillet fried chicken, bourbon and sorghum pecan pie

Ocean Fish Market, 302 Kingston Street, Conway (248-4334)
- whole fried spot, local oysters and fresh shrimp, in season

Ocean One, the Litchfield Inn, One Norris Drive, Pawleys Island (235-8700)
- blue crab cake, barbecue duck eggroll, chicken fried quail with grits, she-crab soup, brown sugar and soy glazed grilled duck breast, pistachio and ginger crusted grouper with blue crab basil sauce

Pine Lakes Tavern, 5201 North Kings Highway, Myrtle Beach (449-4758)
- she-crab soup, crab dip, pimento cheese, Carolina pulled pork, rice and beans, cheddar grits

River Room Restaurant, 801 Front Street, waterfront, Georgetown (527-4110)
- shrimp and grits, crab-stuffed grouper, red beans and rice, soft-shell crab, fried seafood platter, black-eyed pea cakes, spicy crawfish dip, crab cakes, collards, sautéed pound cake, bread pudding with bourbon cream sauce

Rivertown Bistro, 1111 Third Avenue, Conway (248-3733)
- hot crab dip, lump crab cake, fried pork tenderloin, pecan-encrusted catfish, pan-roasted duck breast, brown sugar pound cake

Russell's Seafood Grill and Raw Bar, 4906 U.S. 17 Business, Murrells Inlet (651-0553)
- hogfish, triggerfish, grouper, shrimp platters, she-crab soup and Sarah Gary's incredible hushpuppies

Sea Captain's House, 3002 North Ocean Boulevard, Myrtle Beach (448-8082)
- crab and shrimp omelet, she-crab soup, oyster stew, crab dip, crab cakes, crab casserole, shrimp and grits, seafood platter

Vintage Twelve, 9800 Queensway Boulevard, Myrtle Beach (497-7300)
- butternut squash soup, roasted corn hush puppies, pimento cheese, lump crab cake, pickled shrimp salad, cast-iron pork tenderloin, shrimp and grits

WaterScapes, Marina Inn at Grande Dunes, 8121 Amalfi Place, Myrtle Beach (913-2845)
- shrimp and crab omelet, shrimp salad, pimento cheese, blue crab bisque, collards, Carolina Gold Rice, lump crab cakes and pork belly with fried green tomatoes, smoked blackberries and sorghum glaze

MAMA JANE'S CANDY YAMS

Jane Goings, Georgetown

1–2 pounds sweet potatoes, peeled and sliced
2 cups sugar
1 stick butter or margarine
1 tablespoon cinnamon
1 cup light brown sugar
1 teaspoon nutmeg
2 tablespoons butter nut flavoring
1 tablespoon vanilla flavoring

Put potatoes in a medium-size saucepan. Add remaining ingredients and do not add any water. Cook on the stovetop over very low heat until the potatoes are tender. Do not stir!

MR. NATHANIEL GREEN'S CORNBREAD

Aunny's Country Kitchen, Georgetown

The late Mr. Nathaniel Green owned a few Georgetown restaurants. His memory, through his cornbread, lives on at Aunny's.

2 cups self-rising flour
1 cup self-rising buttermilk cornmeal mix
1 cup sugar
2 eggs
½ can (6 ounces) evaporated milk
1 stick butter or margarine
½ teaspoon baking powder
½ cup water, approximately
2–4 drops yellow food coloring, optional

In a mixing bowl, combine all ingredients, except food coloring, and add water to achieve correct consistency. It should be smooth and slightly thick—not too runny. Whisk until the batter is smooth and no lumps remain. Add food coloring, if desired. Fill muffin cups about halfway. Bake at 350 degrees for about 15 minutes, until tops are slightly golden brown. Makes 3 dozen regular-sized muffins.

Chapter 21
FOR-SPECIAL FOODS

Before there were holidays such as Christmas, Independence Day and Thanksgiving, the first Americans celebrated milestones such as the end of harvest with special ceremonies and feasts. Those feasts may have been modest by modern standards, but one constant that remains in today's holiday meals is an abundance of wild game and seafood. Native Americans hunted ducks and turkeys and gathered seafood, and through the generations, South Carolina natives have enjoyed spending the days before Thanksgiving and Christmas hunting fowl and securing oysters for oyster pies with saltine crusts or for oyster dressing tucked into a bird's cavity.

A nineteenth-century antebellum Christmas breakfast at Chicora Plantation included "sausage, and hogs-head cheese, and hominy, and buckwheat cakes, and honey and waffles, and marmalade, which mamma made from the oranges which grew all round the piazza," wrote Bessie Pringle, who said that their Christmas celebrations lasted for three days. "There was much feasting at Christmas, for a beef and several hogs were always killed and extra rations of sugar, coffee, molasses, and flour were given out, and great quantities of sweet potatoes. Altogether, it was a joyful time."

If there was an additional small hog, it might be butchered right before Christmas so the family and their holiday guests could enjoy the treat of fresh pork. After electricity came and there were freezers, beef roasts became favorite Christmas centerpieces.

Cakes were baked aplenty for holidays, and they still are. Many traditional southern cakes have no frosting, or the frosting was put only between layers

Cakes didn't always have icing on the tops or sides. *Photo circa 1930–50 by William Van Auken Greene. William Van Auken Greene Collection, Horry County Museum, Conway, South Carolina.*

and not on the sides or top. La-Ruth Jordan, who provides delicious crackle-edge lemon pound cake for Freshwater Fish Company north of Conway, bakes about two dozen moist fruitcakes to give to friends and take to parties at Christmastime.

Barbara Whitley is a renowned southern baker who is a partner at Crady's Eclectic Cuisine in Conway. Every year at Christmastime, she starts baking well in advance to fill orders for her uniquely moist fruitcake that's an old family recipe.

Sarah Gary, who has worked in Murrells Inlet–area restaurants most of her life and still, at age seventy-three, preps and cooks food at Russell's Seafood Grill and Raw Bar, said that when she was growing up, the only dessert she recalls having on special occasions is pound cake and ice cream. "Just plain pound cake," she said. "I don't remember any butter or lemon pound cake back then."

"Banana pudding used to be a big thing on Sundays in the black community," said Charles Johnson of Georgetown. "And bread pudding. There was no sauce on bread pudding when I was young. I think they were messing it up by putting sauce on it."

"At Christmastime, we had pumpkin pie [and] sweet potato pies," said Levon Hucks, who grew up on an Horry County tobacco farm. "My mother made a certain kind of fruitcake called a packed fruitcake. We always looked forward to that. She baked it in the oven in a pan, and every ten minutes, she would stir it. When it got cooked to a certain level, she packed it into a tin, sprinkled a little grape juice on top to keep it moist. It would solidify and become almost like a cheesecake, but with fruit, raisins, coconut, pecans, walnuts and pineapple mixed in with it. Maybe on top, little cherries."

Mary Ellen Todd Nance of Myrtle Beach was seventy-one years old on December 16, 1965, when the *Sun News* published an interview with her about how her family celebrated Christmas around 1900 on their farm, located at present-day Thirteenth Avenue South. The article notes their family had fresh pork, "backbone and rice, sweet potatoes, homemade biscuits and fresh fruit," and added that their fresh apples, oranges and occasional bananas were a holiday treat. They raised sugar cane, and during the winter, they "made about 100 gallons of candy, which we pulled until it was almost white. Then, we cut it into small sticks."

Pulitzer Prize–winning author Julia Mood Peterkin (1880–1961) wrote about plantation life in her books and articles. In her famous novel *Scarlet Sister Mary*, the setting was All Saints Parish near Murrells Inlet. In 1934, Peterkin published a slim book called *A Plantation Christmas* that eloquently describes holiday dining at a time right before modern technology changed centuries-old traditions:

Our Christmas preparations begin as soon as Thanksgiving is over, when the Christmas cakes are baked and put away to ripen, with oiled paper wrapped carefully around them to hold the delicious flavor of the scuppernong wine which has been carefully poured all over their dark brown crusts... The pantry shelves already hold rows of jars filled with jellies and jams and pickles and preserves made of figs and peaches and apples and watermelon rinds, and every other fruit and vegetable the garden and orchard yield. Bottles of red and white juices made of berries and grapes stand in colorful and tempting array until they are ready to be used...

Long strands of red peppers hang to nails outside the kitchen door, ready to season the Christmas turkey dressing. Store-bought pepper is hot enough, but it lacks the flavor which these home-grown peppers give, not only to the turkey dressing and the game which the hunters bring in, but to the links of sausage which will soon be strung across the smokehouse and the piles of rich liver pudding in which rice and corn meal both furnish a large share...

The sugar-cane mills scattered over the place cannot finish all their work by daylight and their bright fires make shining red stars at night, while the fragrance of the boiling sirup steams up from the brown gallons which simmer and thicken in the wood-lined vats, promising molasses cake and delicious candy and the best sirup that was ever poured over hot waffles.

The sweet potatoes are in banks, the hay is in stacks, the corn is in the barns, most of the cotton has been picked...

Paper bags threaten to burst and spill the loads of fruit and candy and cakes they are given to hold. The scent of coffee newly parched and ground smothers the pleasant smell of the bunches of bananas which swing from the ceiling and the rank scent of the dried herring in their stained slatted boxes...The restaurant next door flaps its red-and-white calico curtains and sends out inviting odors of catfish and rice...In a pit at one side of the restaurant's yard, a barbecued pig drips sizzling fat on the coals which have cooked it so done and brown. Barbecue sandwiches made of pork and slices of store-bought bread rival the catfish and rice as a welcome change from the food eaten every day...

A festival without feasting would be an empty thing, and the hunters all go out for game. Doves and partridges are plentiful, the big wild ducks have come to spend the winter in the swamps where the sweet gums, drunk on the warmth of the mild winter sunshine, scatter leaves in bright showers of purple and gold with every stir of the wind, hiding the deer tracks which mingle with those of turkeys and wildcats and foxes and raccoons.

The packed fruitcake Levon Hucks remembered his mother making is extremely similar to the one described by Julia Peterkin. He shared that old holiday tradition in his mother's memory.

PACKED FRUITCAKE

Maxine James Hucks, western Horry County

2 cups sugar
¾ cup butter
¼ cup Crisco or lard
½ pound coconut, grated
3 pounds raisins
2–3 pounds nuts, chopped
maraschino cherries (desired amount)
1 small can crushed pineapple, drained
4 cups self-rising flour, divided
5 eggs
1 cup cream
2 tablespoons vanilla
yellow food coloring, if desired

Mix dry ingredients and 1 cup of flour. Stir liquid ingredients together and mix with dry, then add remaining 3 cups flour. Bake in shallow pan at 350 degrees. Stir every 5 minutes until done. It's done when light brown. Don't cook it until it's dry because if you do it won't pack together.

Pack it in an aluminum foil–lined metal tin, without the lid on, until cool. Drizzle with a little grape juice to keep it moist. Cover tin and refrigerate until ready to use if you're not going to use it within a couple of days. Let it come up to room temperature before serving.

SOURCES

CHAPTER 1

Abercrombie, Benjamin. Personal interview by Becky Billingsley. Loris, March 4, 2013.

Brockington, Lee. Personal interview by Becky Billingsley. Georgetown, March 20, 2013.

Hatcher, Harold D. "Buster." Personal interview by Becky Billingsley. Conway, January 8, 2013.

Hill, Walter. Personal interview by Becky Billingsley. Conway, February 18, 2013.

South Carolina Information Highway. "South Carolina—Indians, Native Americans—Indian Tribes," 2012. http://www.sciway.net/hist/indians/tribes.html.

Strickland, Clyde. Telephone interview by Becky Billingsley. Myrtle Beach, April 4, 2013.

CHAPTER 2

Brockington, Lee. Personal interview by Becky Billingsley. Georgetown, March 20, 2013.

D'Anghiera, Pietro Martire. *De Orbe Novo: The Eight Decades of Peter Martyr D'Anghiera*. Google Play edition. New York: G.P. Putnam's Sons, 1912.

Hatcher, Harold D. "Buster." Personal interview by Becky Billingsley. Conway, January 8, 2013.

Hill, Walter. Personal interview by Becky Billingsley. Conway, February 18, 2013.

Holloway, Joseph E. "African Crops and Slave Cuisine." California State University Northridge. www.slaveryinamerica.org.

Huguenot Cellars. "Huguenot History," 2013. http://www.huguenotcellars.com/History.php.

Lewis, Catherine H. *Horry County, South Carolina: 1730–1993*. Columbia: University of South Carolina Press, 1998.

Oliver, Sandra L. *Food in Colonial and Federal America*. Westport, CT: Greenwood Press, 2005.

The Papers of Eliza Lucas Pinckney and Harriott Pinckney Horry. Letter from Eliza Lucas Pinckney to George Morley, [1761]. Digital edition. Edited by Constance Schulz. Charlottesville: University of Virginia Press, Rotunda, 2012. http://rotunda.upress.virginia.edu/PinckneyHorry/ELP0863.

Pringle, Elizabeth W. Allston. *Chronicles of Chicora Wood*. New York: Charles Scribner's Sons, 1922.

Ragsdale, John G. *Dutch Ovens Chronicled: Their Use in the United States*. Fayetteville: University of Arkansas Press, 1991.

Skipper, Wayne. Personal interview by Becky Billingsley. Conway, February 21, 2013.

South Carolina Information Highway. "The African Slave Trade and South Carolina," 2013. http://www.sciway.net/hist/chicora/slavery18-2.html.

Vereen, Sam, and Russell Vereen. Personal interview by Becky Billingsley. Murrells Inlet, March 14, 2013.

CHAPTER 3

Barker-Benfield, G.J., and Catherine Clinton. *American Women from Settlement to the Present*. New York: Oxford University Press, 1998.

Covey, Herbert C., and Dwight Eisnach. *What the Slaves Ate: Recollections of African American Foods and Foodways from the Slave Narratives*. Santa Barbara, CA: Greenwood Press, 2009.

Hatcher, Harold D. "Buster." Personal interview by Becky Billingsley. Conway, January 8, 2013.

Hill, Walter. Personal interview by Becky Billingsley. Conway, February 18, 2013.

Hooker, Richard J. Introduction to *A Colonial Plantation Cookbook: The Receipt Book of Harriott Pinckney Horry, 1770*. Columbia: University of South Carolina Press, 1984.

Horry, Harriott Pinckney. *A Colonial Plantation Cookbook: The Receipt Book of Harriott Pinckney Horry, 1770*. Edited by and with an introduction by Richard J. Hooker. Columbia: University of South Carolina Press, 1984.

Joyner, Charles. *Down by the Riverside: A South Carolina Slave Community*. Urbana: University of Illinois Press, 1984.

Mills, Kincaid, Genevieve C. Peterkin and Aaron McCollough. *Coming Through: Voices of a South Carolina Gullah Community from WPA Oral Histories Collected by Genevieve W. Chandler*. Columbia: University of South Carolina Press, 2008.

National Park Service. "Rice Cultivation in Georgetown County," 2013. www.nps.gov/nr/twhp/wwwlps/lessons/3rice/3facts1.htm.

The Papers of Eliza Lucas Pinckney and Harriott Pinckney Horry. "A Common Bread Pudding." Digital edition. Edited by Constance Schulz. Charlottesville: University of Virginia Press, Rotunda, 2012. http://rotunda.upress. virginia.edu/PinckneyHorry/ELP1299.

———. Eliza Lucas Pinckney to Fanny Fayerweather, [1741]. Digital edition. Edited by Constance Schulz. Charlottesville: University of Virginia Press, Rotunda, 2012. http://rotunda.upress.virginia.edu/PinckneyHorry/ ELP0948.

———. Eliza Lucas Pinckney to George Lucas, June 4, 1741. Digital edition. Edited by Constance Schulz. Charlottesville: University of Virginia Press, Rotunda, 2012. http://rotunda.upress.virginia.edu/PinckneyHorry/ ELP0878.

———. Eliza Lucas Pinckney to George Lucas, [1744]. Digital edition. Edited by Constance Schulz. Charlottesville: University of Virginia Press, Rotunda, 2012. http://rotunda.upress.virginia.edu/PinckneyHorry/ ELP0813.

———. Eliza Lucas Pinckney to Mary Bartlett, [1742]. Digital edition. Edited by Constance Schulz. Charlottesville: University of Virginia Press, Rotunda, 2012. http://rotunda.upress.virginia.edu/PinckneyHorry/ ELP0115.

———. Eliza Lucas Pinckney to Mary Steer (Mrs. Richard) Boddicott, 2 May [1740]. Digital edition. Edited by Constance Schulz. Charlottesville: University of Virginia Press, Rotunda, 2012. http://rotunda.upress. virginia.edu/PinckneyHorry/ELP0152.

———. Eliza Lucas Pinckney to Thomas Lucas, May 22, 1742. Digital edition. Edited by Constance Schulz. Charlottesville: University of Virginia Press, Rotunda, 2012. http://rotunda.upress.virginia.edu/ PinckneyHorry/ELP0383.

———. Harriott Pinckney Horry, 1815 Journal, May 28, 1815. Digital edition. Edited by Constance Schulz. Charlottesville: University of Virginia Press, Rotunda, 2012. http://rotunda.upress.virginia.edu/PinckneyHorry/ELP1064.

———. Harriott Pinckney Horry, 1793 Journal, November 23 and 24, 1793. Digital edition. Edited by Constance Schulz. Charlottesville: University of Virginia Press, Rotunda, 2012. http://rotunda.upress.virginia.edu/PinckneyHorry/ELP1411.

———. Lord Charles Montague and Elizabeth Balmer Montague (Lady Charles) to Eliza Lucas Pinckney, n.d. Digital edition. Edited by Constance Schulz. Charlottesville: University of Virginia Press, Rotunda, 2012. http://rotunda.upress.virginia.edu/PinckneyHorry/ELP0290.

———. "To Make Westphalian Hamms." Digital edition. Edited by Constance Schulz. Charlottesville: University of Virginia Press, Rotunda, 2012. http://rotunda.upress.virginia.edu/PinckneyHorry/ELP1335.

———. "To Pickle Mackerel Calld Ceveechd." Digital edition. Edited by Constance Schulz. Charlottesville: University of Virginia Press, Rotunda, 2012. http://rotunda.upress.virginia.edu/PinckneyHorry/ELP1298.

———. "To Preserve Apricots Whole." Digital edition. Edited by Constance Schulz. Charlottesville: University of Virginia Press, Rotunda, 2012. http://rotunda.upress.virginia.edu/PinckneyHorry/ELP1301.

———. "To Recover Veal When It Has Grown Sower." Digital edition. Edited by Constance Schulz. Charlottesville: University of Virginia Press, Rotunda, 2012. http://rotunda.upress.virginia.edu/PinckneyHorry/ELP1308.

Pringle, Elizabeth W. Allston. *Chronicles of Chicora Wood*. New York: Charles Scribner's Sons, 1922.

Rutledge, Sarah. *The Carolina Housewife*. Columbia: University of South Carolina Press, 1979.

Schulze, Richard. *Carolina Gold Rice: The Ebb and Flow History of a Lowcountry Cash Crop*. Charleston, SC: The History Press, 2005.

South Carolina Information Highway. "The Lives of African-American Slaves in Carolina During the 18th Century," 2013. http://www.sciway.net/hist/chicora/slavery18-3.html.

Talbert, Roy, Jr. "So Fine a Beach: Peter Horry's Summer of 1812." Paper presented at the Coastal Carolina University Distinguished Teacher-Scholar Lecturer Series, Conway, South Carolina, October 1, 1998.

Chapter 4

Barker-Benfield, G.J., and Catherine Clinton. *American Women from Settlement to the Present*. New York: Oxford University Press, 1998.

Gantt, Jesse Edward, Jr., and Veronica Davis Gerald. *The Ultimate Gullah Cookbook*. South Carolina: Gullah House Foundation, 2003.

Goings, Jane. Personal interview by Becky Billingsley. Georgetown, February 28, 2013.

Holloway, Joseph E. "African Crops and Slave Cuisine." California State University Northridge. www.slaveryinamerica.org.

Hooker, Richard J. Introduction to *A Colonial Plantation Cookbook: The Receipt Book of Harriott Pinckney Horry, 1770*. Columbia: University of South Carolina Press, 1984.

Hucks, Levon. Personal interview by Becky Billingsley. Conway, February 2, 2013.

Johnson, Aun. Personal interview by Becky Billingsley. Georgetown, January 7, 2013.

Johnson, Benjamin "B.B." Personal interview by Becky Billingsley. Georgetown, January 10, 2013.

Johnson, Charles. Personal interview by Becky Billingsley. Georgetown, January 7, 2013.

Joyner, Charles. *Down by the Riverside: A South Carolina Slave Community*. Urbana: University of Illinois Press, 1984.

Library of Congress. "Are Black-Eyed Peas Really Peas?" 2013. http://www.loc.gov/rr/scitech/mysteries/blackeyedpeas.html.

Nature Conservancy. "Sandy Island Preserve," 2013. http://www.nature.org/ourinitiatives/regions/northamerica/unitedstates/southcarolina/placesweprotect/sandy-island-preserve.xml.

Oliver, Sandra L. *Food in Colonial and Federal America*. Westport, CT: Greenwood Press, 2005.

S.C. Department of Agriculture. "SC Watermelon History," 2013. http://agriculture.sc.gov/Watermelon/history.

Simmons, Amelia. *The First American Cookbook: A Facsimile of 'American Cookery,' 1796*. New York: Dover Publications Inc., 1984.

Skipper, Wayne. Personal interview by Becky Billingsley. Conway, February 21, 2013.

South Carolina's Information Highway. "South Carolina Plantations, Sandy Island, South Carolina," 2013. http://south-carolina-plantations.com/georgetown/sandy-island-sc-plantations.html.

Stradley, Linda. What's Cooking America. "History of Collard Greens," 2013. http://whatscookingamerica.net/Vegetables/CollardGreens.htm.

CHAPTER 5

Bartram, William. *Travels Through North & South Carolina, Georgia, East & West Florida, the Cherokee Country, the Extensive Territories of the Muscogulges, or Creek Confederacy, and the Country of the Chactaws; Containing an Account of the Soil and Natural Productions of Those Regions, Together with Observations on the Manners of the Indians*. Digital edition. Chapel Hill: University of North Carolina, 2001.

Brockington, Lee G., and Linwood Altman. *Pawleys Island: A Century of History and Photographs.* Charleston, SC: Joggling Board Press & Evening Post Publishing Company, 2008.

Curtis, Becky Ward. Personal interview by Becky Billingsley. Georgetown, January 30, 2013.

Fitch, James A. *Pass the Pileau, Please.* Georgetown, SC: self-published, 2001.

Hatcher, Bob Lee. Personal interview by Becky Billingsley. Aynor, February 16, 2013.

Hill, Walter. Personal interview by Becky Billingsley. Conway, February 18, 2013.

Lewis, Catherine H. *Horry County, South Carolina: 1730–1993.* Columbia: University of South Carolina Press, 1998.

Schulze, Richard. *Carolina Gold Rice: The Ebb and Flow History of a Lowcountry Cash Crop.* Charleston, SC: The History Press, 2005.

Skipper, Wayne. Personal interview by Becky Billingsley. Conway, February 2, 2013.

Strickland, Clyde. Telephone interview by Becky Billingsley. Myrtle Beach, April 4, 2013.

Chapter 6

Day, Ivan. Historic Food. "Syllabubs and Possets," 2003. http://www.historicfood.com/Syllabub%20Recipes.htm.

The Papers of Eliza Lucas Pinckney and Harriott Pinckney Horry. Charles Cotesworth Pinckney (1746–1825) to Eliza Lucas Pinckney, September 14, 1780. Digital edition. Edited by Constance Schulz. Charlottesville: University of Virginia Press, Rotunda, 2012. http://rotunda.upress.virginia.edu/PinckneyHorry/ELP0257.

————. Daniel Huger Horry Jr., Accounts Audited of Claims Growing Out of the Revolution, June 25, 1783. Digital edition. Edited by Constance Schulz. Charlottesville: University of Virginia Press, Rotunda, 2012. http://rotunda.upress.virginia.edu/PinckneyHorry/ELP0231.

————. Thomas Pinckney (1750–1828) to Eliza Lucas Pinckney, September 7, 1780. Digital edition. Edited by Constance Schulz. Charlottesville: University of Virginia Press, Rotunda, 2012. http://rotunda.upress.virginia.edu/PinckneyHorry/ELP0522.

————. Thomas Pinckney (1750–1828) to Harriott Pinckney Horry, April 19, 1779. Digital edition. Edited by Constance Schulz. Charlottesville: University of Virginia Press, Rotunda, 2012. http://rotunda.upress.virginia.edu/PinckneyHorry/ELP0522.

————. Thomas Pinckney (1750–1828) to Harriott Pinckney Horry, February 1, 1776. Digital edition. Edited by Constance Schulz. Charlottesville: University of Virginia Press, Rotunda, 2012. http://rotunda.upress.virginia.edu/PinckneyHorry/ELP0487.

————. Thomas Pinckney (1750–1828) to Harriott Pinckney Horry, January 31, 1777. Digital edition. Edited by Constance Schulz. Charlottesville: University of Virginia Press, Rotunda, 2012. http://rotunda.upress.virginia.edu/PinckneyHorry/ELP0515.

————. Thomas Pinckney (1750–1828) to Harriott Pinckney Horry, July 31, 1777. Digital edition. Edited by Constance Schulz. Charlottesville: University of Virginia Press, Rotunda, 2012. http://rotunda.upress.virginia.edu/PinckneyHorry/ELP0521.

————. Thomas Pinckney (1750–1828) to Harriott Pinckney Horry, May 23, 1778. Digital edition. Edited by Constance Schulz. Charlottesville: University of Virginia Press, Rotunda, 2012. http://rotunda.upress.virginia.edu/PinckneyHorry/ELP0522.

————. Thomas Pinckney (1750–1828) to Harriott Pinckney Horry, November 2, 1775. Digital edition. Edited by Constance Schulz. Charlottesville: University of Virginia Press, Rotunda, 2012. http://rotunda.upress.virginia.edu/PinckneyHorry/ELP0485.

———. Thomas Pinckney (1750–1828) to Harriott Pinckney Horry, September 15, 1777. Digital edition. Edited by Constance Schulz. Charlottesville: University of Virginia Press, Rotunda, 2012. http://rotunda.upress.virginia.edu/PinckneyHorry/ELP0522.

———. Thomas Pinckney (1750–1828) to Harriott Pinckney Horry, September 7, 1780. Digital edition. Edited by Constance Schulz. Charlottesville: University of Virginia Press, Rotunda, 2012. http://rotunda.upress.virginia.edu/PinckneyHorry/ELP0522.

Simms, William Gilmore. *The Life of Francis Marion.* eBook edition. Project Gutenberg, 2013. http://www.gutenberg.org/catalog/world/readfile?fk_files=3304479.

CHAPTER 7

Grizzard, Frank E. *George Washington: A Biographical Companion.* Digital edition. Santa Barbara, CA: ABC-CLIO, 2002.

Hill, Walter. Personal interview by Becky Billingsley. Conway, February 18, 2013.

Kinder, Cindy. Personal interview by Becky Billingsley. Georgetown, February 28, 2013.

Lewis, Catherine. "Little River." Horry County Historical Society Online, 1999. http://www.hchsonline.org/places/littleriver.html.

Oliver, Sandra L. *Food in Colonial and Federal America.* Westport, CT: Greenwood Press, 2005.

The Papers of Eliza Lucas Pinckney and Harriott Pinckney Horry. Harriott Pinckney Horry to George Washington, April 14, 1791. Digital edition. Edited by Constance Schulz. Charlottesville: University of Virginia Press, Rotunda, 2012. http://rotunda.upress.virginia.edu/PinckneyHorry/ELP0842.

———. John Rutledge to Thomas Pinckney (1750–1828), [April 28,] 1791. Digital edition. Edited by Constance Schulz. Charlottesville: University of Virginia Press, Rotunda, 2012. http://rotunda.upress.virginia.edu/PinckneyHorry/ELP0104.

Pringle, Elizabeth W. Allston. *Chronicles of Chicora Wood*. New York: Charles Scribner's Sons, 1922.

Salmon, Robin. E-mail interview by Becky Billingsley. April 27, 2013.

South Carolina Information Highway. "South Carolina—History of South Carolina Tea Farms," 2013. http://www.sciway.net/hist/indians/tribes.html.

Vereen, Russell. Personal interview by Becky Billingsley. Murrells Inlet, March 11, 2013.

Vereen, Sam, and Russell Vereen. Personal interview by Becky Billingsley. Murrells Inlet, March 14, 2013.

Washington, George. *The Diary of George Washington, from 1789 to 1791.* Edited by Benson J. Lossing. Digital edition. Richmond, VA: Press of the Historical Society, 1861.

CHAPTER 8

Bock, Gordon. "History of the Kitchen Stove." Old House Online, 2013. http://www.oldhouseonline.com/history-of-the-kitchen-stove.

Hill, Walter. Personal interview by Becky Billingsley. Conway, February 18, 2013.

Hooker, Richard J. Introduction to *A Colonial Plantation Cookbook: The Receipt Book of Harriott Pinckney Horry, 1770.* Columbia: University of South Carolina Press, 1984.

Lewis, Catherine H. *Horry County, South Carolina: 1730–1993*. Columbia: University of South Carolina Press, 1998.

Lewis, J.D. "South Carolina—The War of 1812." Carolana, 2007. http://www.carolana.com/SC/1800s/antebellum/war_of_1812.html.

Martin, Greg. "The Ark Plantation." Horry County Historical Society, 1999. http://www.hchsonline.org/places/ark.html.

Oliver, Sandra L. *Food in Colonial and Federal America*. Westport, CT: Greenwood Press, 2005.

The Papers of Eliza Lucas Pinckney and Harriott Pinckney Horry. Charles Cotesworth Pinckney (1746–1825) to William F. Behr, August 26, 1813. Digital edition. Edited by Constance Schulz. Charlottesville: University of Virginia Press, Rotunda, 2012. http://rotunda.upress.virginia.edu/PinckneyHorry/ELP0138.

———. Daniel (Charles Lucas Pinckney) Horry to Harriott Pinckney Horry, October 8 and 11, 1807. Digital edition. Edited by Constance Schulz. Charlottesville: University of Virginia Press, Rotunda, 2012. http://rotunda.upress.virginia.edu/PinckneyHorry/ELP0550.

———. Eleanore de la Tour-Maubourg Horry and Daniel (Charles Lucas Pinckney) Horry to Harriott Pinckney Horry, September 8, 1806. Digital edition. Edited by Constance Schulz. Charlottesville: University of Virginia Press, Rotunda, 2012. http://rotunda.upress.virginia.edu/PinckneyHorry/ELP0476.

———. Thomas Pinckney (1750–1828) to Harriott Pinckney Horry, December 6, 1822. Digital edition. Edited by Constance Schulz. Charlottesville: University of Virginia Press, Rotunda, 2012. http://rotunda.upress.virginia.edu/PinckneyHorry/ELP0633.

———. Thomas Pinckney (1750–1828) to Harriott Pinckney Horry, January 24, 1814. Digital edition. Edited by Constance Schulz. Charlottesville: University of Virginia Press, Rotunda, 2012. http://rotunda.upress.virginia.edu/PinckneyHorry/ELP0610.

————. Thomas Pinckney (1750–1828) to Harriott Pinckney Horry, July 1, 1824. Digital edition. Edited by Constance Schulz. Charlottesville: University of Virginia Press, Rotunda, 2012. http://rotunda.upress. virginia.edu/PinckneyHorry/ELP0640.

Pringle, Elizabeth W. Allston. *Chronicles of Chicora Wood*. New York: Charles Scribner's Sons, 1922.

Stubbs, William C., AM, PhD. "Cultivation of Sugar Cane," *Morning News Print*, 1900.

Talbert, Roy, Jr. "So Fine a Beach: Peter Horry's Summer of 1812." Paper presented at the Coastal Carolina University Distinguished Teacher-Scholar Lecturer Series, Conway, South Carolina, October 1, 1998.

CHAPTER 9

Joyner, Charles. Introduction to *A Woman Rice Planter*. Columbia: University of South Carolina Press in cooperation with the Institute for Southern Studies and the South Carolina Society, 1992.

Lewis, Catherine H. *Horry County, South Carolina: 1730–1993*. Columbia: University of South Carolina Press, 1998.

Pringle, Elizabeth W. Allston. *Chronicles of Chicora Wood*. New York: Charles Scribner's Sons, 1922.

West & Johnson Publishers. *Confederate Receipt Book: A Compilation of Over One Hundred Receipts, Adapted to the Times*. Richmond, VA: G.W. Gary, 1863. Electronic edition by the University of North Carolina–Chapel Hill and the Institute of Museum and Library Services, 1999. http://docsouth. unc.edu/imls/receipt/receipt.html.

CHAPTER 10

Brockington, Lee G., and Linwood Altman. *Pawleys Island: A Century of History and Photographs.* Charleston, SC: Joggling Board Press & Evening Post Publishing Company, 2008.

Hill, Walter. Personal interview by Becky Billingsley. Conway, February 18, 2013.

Pringle, Elizabeth Allston (Patience Pennington). *A Woman Rice Planter.* New York: Macmillan, 1913.

CHAPTER 11

Bourne, Jack. E-mail interview by Becky Billingsley. Myrtle Beach, April 8–12, 2013.

———. "Myrtle Beach History, 1905 to 2005," 2008. http://www.youtube.com/watch?v=KrIuipa3zAs.

———. "Myrtle Beach Ocean Forest Hotel, 1930–1974," 2008. http://www.youtube.com/watch?v=P-WlBM6Vwgw.

Brockington, Lee G. Personal interview by Becky Billingsley. Georgetown, March 20, 2013.

———. *Plantation Between the Waters: A Brief History of Hobcaw Barony.* Charleston, SC: The History Press, 2006.

Brockington, Lee G., and Linwood Altman. *Pawleys Island: A Century of History and Photographs.* Charleston, SC: Joggling Board Press & Evening Post Publishing Company, 2008.

Camlin, Donald Williams. Personal interview by Becky Billingsley. Georgetown, January 30, 2013.

Curtis, Becky Ward. Personal interview by Becky Billingsley. Georgetown, January 30, 2013.

The Department of Agriculture, Commerce and Industries and Clemson College. *South Carolina: A Handbook*. Columbia, SC: self-published, 1927. Copyright not claimed.

Lewis, Catherine H. *Horry County, South Carolina: 1730–1993*. Columbia: University of South Carolina Press, 1998.

Nance, Clay. Telephone interview by Becky Billingsley. Myrtle Beach, April 29, 2013.

Vermont, Captain Sandy. "The Twentieth Century." Georgetown, South Carolina, 2004. http://www.georgetown-sc.com/history.

CHAPTER 12

Skipper, Wayne. Personal interview by Becky Billingsley. Conway, February 21, 2013.

CHAPTER 13

Bourne, Jack. "Myrtle Beach History, 1905 to 2005," 2008. http://www.youtube.com/watch?v=KrIuipa3zAs.

Brockington, Lee G., and Linwood Altman. *Pawleys Island: A Century of History and Photographs*. Charleston, SC: Joggling Board Press & Evening Post Publishing Company, 2008.

Camlin, Donald Williams. Personal interview by Becky Billingsley. Georgetown, January 30, 2013.

Curtis, Becky Ward. Personal interview by Becky Billingsley. Georgetown, January 30, 2013.

Dorman, Kelly Lee. Personal interview by Becky Billingsley. Murrells Inlet, March 20, 2013.

Gary, Sarah. Personal interview by Becky Billingsley. Murrells Inlet, March 14, 2013.

Hawkins, Maxine Oliver. Personal interview by Becky Billingsley. Murrells Inlet, July 2002.

Lee, Alzata. Personal interview by Becky Billingsley. Murrells Inlet, July 2002.

———. Telephone interview by Becky Billingsley. Murrells Inlet, March 22, 2013.

Nance, Clay. Telephone interview by Becky Billingsley. Myrtle Beach, April 29, 2013.

Thompson, Dino. *Greek Boy Growing Up Southern.* Myrtle Beach, SC: Snug Press, 1999.

———. Personal interview by Becky Billingsley. Myrtle Beach, July 2002.

Vereen, Russell. Personal interview by Becky Billingsley. Murrells Inlet, March 11, 2013.

Vereen, Sam, and Russell Vereen. Personal interview by Becky Billingsley. Murrells Inlet, March 14, 2013.

Yates, Tina. Personal interview by Becky Billingsley. North Myrtle Beach, April 2, 2013.

Chapter 14

Bourne, Jack. E-mail interview by Becky Billingsley. Myrtle Beach, April 8–12, 2013.

————. "Mom and Pop Inns Along Myrtle Beach's Grand Strand," 2008. http://www.youtube.com/watch?v=cATNkIPMYmo.

Camlin, Donald Williams. Personal interview by Becky Billingsley. Georgetown, January 30, 2013.

CNN Money. "10 Fastest-Growing Cities: Myrtle Beach, S.C." March 28, 2011. http://money.cnn.com/galleries/2011/real_estate/1103/gallery. Fastest_growing_metro_areas/9.html.

Cribb, Jean. Interview by Becky Billingsley. Personal interview. Myrtle Beach, July 2002.

Curtis, Becky Ward. Personal interview by Becky Billingsley. Georgetown, January 30, 2013.

Dorman, Kelly Lee. Personal interview by Becky Billingsley. Murrells Inlet, July 2002.

Drosas, Dino. Interview by Becky Billingsley. Personal interview. Myrtle Beach, July 2002.

Eshleman, Tom. E-mail interview by Becky Billingsley. Myrtle Beach, April 1, 2013.

Nance, Clay. Telephone interview by Becky Billingsley. Myrtle Beach, April 29, 2013.

Thompson, Dino. Personal interview by Becky Billingsley. Myrtle Beach, July 2002.

Vereen, Russell. Personal interview by Becky Billingsley. Murrells Inlet, March 11, 2013.

CHAPTER 15

Leithiser, Jon. Personal interview by Becky Billingsley. Loris, March 4, 2013.

CHAPTER 16

Brockington, Lee. Personal interview by Becky Billingsley. Georgetown, March 20, 2013.

CHAPTER 17

Holloway, Joseph E. "African Crops and Slave Cuisine." California State University Northridge. www.slaveryinamerica.org.

Hucks, Levon. Personal interview by Becky Billingsley. Conway, February 2, 2013.

Johnson, Benjamin "B.B." Personal interview by Becky Billingsley. Georgetown, January 10, 2013.

Johnson, Charles. Personal interview by Becky Billingsley. Georgetown, January 7, 2013.

Pringle, Elizabeth Allston (Patience Pennington). *A Woman Rice Planter.* New York: Macmillan, 1913.

Rutledge, Sarah. *The Carolina Housewife.* Columbia: University of South Carolina Press, 1979.

Skipper, Wayne. Personal interview by Becky Billingsley. Conway, February 21, 2013.

Smith, Andrew. *Peanuts: The Illustrious History of the Goober Pea.* Urbana: University of Illinois Press, 2002.

CHAPTER 18

Johnson, Aun. Personal interview by Becky Billingsley. Georgetown, January 7, 2013.

Johnson, Charles. Personal interview by Becky Billingsley. Georgetown, January 7, 2013.

Lee, Alzata. Personal interview by Becky Billingsley. Murrells Inlet, July 2002.

CHAPTER 19

Brockington, Lee. Personal interview by Becky Billingsley. Georgetown, March 20, 2013.

Camlin, Donald Williams. Personal interview by Becky Billingsley. Georgetown, January 30, 2013.

Capps, Leona. Personal interview by Becky Billingsley. Conway, October 1998.

Curtis, Becky Ward. Personal interview by Becky Billingsley. Georgetown, January 30, 2013.

Johnson, Aun. Personal interview by Becky Billingsley. Georgetown, January 7, 2013.

Johnson, Benjamin "B.B." Personal interview by Becky Billingsley. Georgetown, January 10, 2013.

Johnson, Charles. Personal interview by Becky Billingsley. Georgetown, January 7, 2013.

Osteen, Louis. *Louis Osteen's Charleston Cuisine: Recipes from a Lowcountry Chef*. Chapel Hill, NC: Algonquin Books of Chapel Hill, 1999.

———. Personal interview by Becky Billingsley. Pawleys Island, January 3, 2013.

South Carolina Department of Natural Resources. "Freshwater Turtles," 2013. http://www.dnr.sc.gov/cwcs/pdf/FreshwaterTurtles.pdf.

South Carolina Information Highway. "South Carolina State Reptile—Loggerhead Sea Turtle," 2013. http://www.sciway.net/facts/sc-state-reptile-loggerhead-turtle.html.

Chapter 21

Gary, Sarah. Personal interview by Becky Billingsley. Murrells Inlet, March 14, 2013.

Hucks, Levon. Personal interview by Becky Billingsley. Conway, February 2, 2013.

Johnson, Benjamin "B.B." Personal interview by Becky Billingsley. Georgetown, January 10, 2013.

Jordan, La-Ruth. Personal interview by Becky Billingsley. Conway, March 14, 2013.

Peterkin, Julia Mood. *A Plantation Christmas*. New York: Books for Libraries Press, 1934.

Pringle, Elizabeth W. Allston. *Chronicles of Chicora Wood*. New York: Charles Scribner's Sons, 1922.

Skipper, Wayne. Personal interview by Becky Billingsley. Conway, February 21, 2013.

INDEX

W

Waccamaw 13, 21, 32, 97, 100
Waccamaw People 13, 15, 20
walnuts 39, 116
War of 1812 56, 69
Washington, George 38, 58, 59
watermelons 32, 45, 71, 88, 107, 113,
        164
Wayside Restaurant 124, 126, 127, 133
wine 24, 32, 33, 39, 57, 60, 74, 83, 92,
        113, 164
winnowing 98
Winyah Bay 13, 20, 69, 90, 152
Winyah Indigo Society 64
World War II 119

Y

yams 25, 40, 44, 157, 161

ABOUT THE AUTHOR

Becky Billingsley was a general features, food and restaurant reporter at the *Sun News* daily newspaper in Myrtle Beach and was the founding editor and journalist for *Coastal Carolina Dining* magazine. At both publications, she wrote about area history, such as renovations of former slave cabins at Hobcaw Barony in Georgetown, President George Washington's 1791 visit to the Grand Strand and local food history and traditions.

Since 2008, Becky has published an annual magazine called *The Top 100 Grand Strand Restaurants* and serves daily information at myrtlebeachrestaurantnews. com. She has written food, restaurant, travel and feature articles for many local, regional and national websites and publications, including *South Carolina Living* magazine, the *Charlotte Observer*, *Litchfield Style* magazine, the *Georgetown Times*, *Weekly Surge* and getawaysforgrowups.com.

Becky lives in the Socastee area of Myrtle Beach with her husband of thirty-two years, Matt, and they have two adult sons. They enjoy bird-watching, boating, visiting historic sites and trying new foods.